BAILING OUT
ON THE
BORDERLINE

Authors Note:

The events, places, and conversations in this memoir have been recreated from memory, journal entries, letters, photographs, and interviews. They are my memories. I understand that others have their own memories which may be different.

Some events have been compressed for the purpose of the story although I wish they had been compressed in life as well.

The names and identifying characteristics of all individuals (except my twin sister who has provided me written permission, my grandmother, and my first hamster, Matilda) and places have been changed to maintain anonymity.

Any perceived slight of any individual or organization is purely unintentional.

Published by Seacoast Press, an imprint of Mindstir Media, LLC
1931 Woodbury Ave. #182 | Portsmouth, NH 03801 | USA
1.800.767.0531 | www.seacoastpress.com

Printed in the United States of America
ISBN-13: 978-1-7334732-1-7

BAILING OUT
ON THE
BORDERLINE

A Memoir of Loving
and Leaving a Spouse with
Borderline Personality Disorder

JULIA SINCLAIR

SEACOAST
PRESS

For all those who have tolerated abusive relationships hoping to make it work and to all those who lost their lives because they didn't make it out in time.

CONTENTS

SECTION 1
CHILDHOOD

CHAPTER 1
BEGINNINGS, VIOLENCE AND LOVE

"Your perspective on life comes from the cage you were held captive in"

– Shannon L. Alder, INSPIRATIONAL AUTHOR

"You goddam good for nothing kids – always thinking of yourselves. Your mother will be home soon and look at this place!" My father was shouting at his youngest children: my brother Brian who was 10, my twin sister, Jennifer and me, just a year younger. We were old enough to remember that our father hadn't always been like this, but since his drinking had got more frequent, and my mother had started working part time in the evenings at a local retail store, he could fly into a rage so easily.

My defenses went up within seconds of my father's anger. Should I fight back or run to my room? It didn't matter which I chose. Both would make my father furious and I would suffer the consequences. Lately, our household could suddenly go from being a safe environment, where we snuggled under blankets watching 'Three's Company', to a battle ground where we were fighting off our father's artillery onslaught.

I quickly scanned the dining room table where my father had pointed and grabbed my math book, just as he was kicking my Barbie doll out of her Mattel fold-out airplane. As the plastic pink seats flew across the room I ran over to grab them too, and my Ken doll, to minimize further damage in Barbie's kingdom. Brian escaped upstairs to the chilly second floor of the house.

Sometimes I would stand up to my father, but I didn't have the guts to swear at him. My sister did. Jennifer followed my father now as he kicked her backpack across the living room, and shouted:

"Goddam yourself Daddy – you're an asshole!"

Her two brown braids swung from side to side as my father turned on her.

"You think you're something special don't you little missy?" He advanced on her menacingly. "Well, I'll show you something, you good-for-nothing kid!" His face was screwed up with rage as he backhanded her, and then punched her in the stomach.

I charged between them to stop him punching Jennifer again, as she lay winded like a rag doll on the floor, and I stared him down.

"Daddy! Stop! Stop!........You are breaking everything!"

Just that morning, my father had been relaxing in his living room chair, listening to Roger Whittaker's "The Last Farewell"; humming along while polishing his guns. Now he was a twisted-face ogre who had just driven his fist into his own daughter, without an ounce of remorse.

I looked out of the window to see my mother pulling into the driveway, coming home from work. She was driving the family car, a light blue 75 Ford Torino station wagon. Jennifer, my father and I all started shouting recriminations as she walked in the door.

"How come it always has to be like this when I get home?" She said, as she let the groceries in her arms cascade onto the kitchen table.

"Mommy, he punched me!" Jennifer cried from the floor.

"He did. He just rammed his fist right into her stomach," I seconded. "Really hard."

My father just stared at our mother and said nothing.

Not for the first time I hoped that my mother would admonish our father and make the violence and shouting end. Instead, she just looked at the books scattered all over the floor.

"Girls, pick up your things," she sighed.

"Marjie, these goddam kids don't lift a finger around here...the house is always a mess....but when they want something you spoil these brats. Cry, cry, cry....that's all these kids do."

It was so unfair and I felt my own anger rise.

"I told you Mommy said it was okay to do my homework at the table. Tell him Mommy!"

But Jennifer spoke before she could: "Mommy, your husband's an asshole!"

Jennifer didn't seem to care if she got another beating. Sometimes I was in awe of my twin. My mother rubbed her head. I knew this meant she was trying to ward off an oncoming migraine.

"Walter, I don't need the house clean if it means this. I am so tired."

"You always have to take the side of the kids, don't you, Marjie?"

He glared at my mother and headed down to his workshop in the basement of the house.

"Look Mommy. Look what he did to me!" Jennifer lifted her shirt to show my mother the angry red mark on her stomach. She would have a terrific bruise.

"Jennifer!" My mother was angry now, but not with our father. With us! "Why do you always have to get him going? Take your stuff and go to your room!"

"But Mommy....."

"Jennifer, just leave your father alone!" my exhausted mother implored.

We knew then we were on our own to endure the emotional and physical assault our father meted out. There wasn't any point in yelling at her.

I felt so sad for my sister. Identical to me in every way, we shared long brown braids, hazel eyes, and freckles. We also shared thoughts and emotions. We even had our own language when we were younger. I knew she needed me to be tougher, and to stand up to our father beside her. But I just didn't feel strong enough or big enough. Yet.

14

***

The following morning I got up early. It was mid winter and I did not want to remain long in the unheated bedroom that I shared with my siblings. Jennifer wasn't yet awake, so I hurried downstairs to sit in front of the wall vent that had warm air blowing out of it, as part of the forced hot air heating system for the first floor.

I heard my father moving around as he got ready for work. I saw him grab his briefcase from a cluttered counter top in the dining room where he had put it the night before.

"Do you have your lunch, Walter?" I heard my mother ask him kindly. Why was she speaking to him so kindly, I wondered, after he had beaten up her nine year-old daughter?

"Yes, dear. I'll see you tonight," my father responded, giving my mother a kiss on the lips.

"Bye, bye!" My mother smiled at him as he went out the front door.

"Mommy?" I said in a low, tired voice.

"Yes, honey?"

"Did Daddy tell you he kicked Barbie's airplane last night?"

"No honey. I put your Barbie and the plane in your room."

"But, Mommy…." Then I stopped. I knew when I saw her counting out three Tylenols and swallowing them that bringing it up again would just make her more upset and make her headache worse.

"Are you okay, Mommy?" I asked.

"Yes, honey. Don't worry. I will be okay."

I was worried about my mother.

I also worried about the fights. What would cause a fight one night, might not the next. One night, having elbows on the table at supper time would set my father off, but on another night it wouldn't be brought up. Another night, everything had kicked off because I answered the telephone.

"Jesus Christ Almighty! These kids are answering the telephone now?" My father screamed at my mother. I had been answering the telephone for as long as I could remember, so I was very confused as to why my father now saw it as significant, and wrong. Why is it suddenly a big deal, I wondered?

A missing television guide could cause World War Three one night, and the next night my father's reaction would be: "Oh dear……….that's just how it goes, now go find your hamster, and see if she would like some of this leftover toast from breakfast."

Then he would gather some food bits together to spoil my first official pet, Matilda. He was the most loving, caring person to small animals all the time, and to his children some of the time.

That unpredictability made one feel as if the ground we were walking on was not secure, as if it could give way at any moment. Even when Daddy was being nice we knew we were only one step away from an outburst, and therefore we could never enjoy the good times, as we never knew how quickly they would end. But sometimes our father and mother could be wonderful. I particularly remember one incident where, looking back, I was probably being an absolute brat, but my father was as loving and kind as it was possible to be.

Having been a majorette for her high school band in the early 50's, my mother loved the idea of having her twin girls learn baton twirling. Without the need for much convincing, Jennifer and I, who were always looking for an adults' approval, agreed to take lessons once a week after school.

The sport of baton twirling was, and continues to be, a form of art in sport, similar to gymnastics or synchronized swimming. My mother enjoyed watching us twirl and we yearned to see her smile.

We practiced twirling our batons together outdoors, and in the basement of our house. My two eldest siblings, who were several years older than us, would engage in their own activities while we practiced. My oldest sister, Debra, who was already 17 when we were nine, was still a junior in high school due to repeating a grade in elementary school. All of her friends were significantly younger than she was, but she enjoyed socializing with that age group more than her own. She was a loner; tall and lanky, she walked with her shoulders forward in order to try to look shorter. Debra had a difficult time fitting in, but she would spend hours dribbling a basketball while Jennifer and I practiced our twirling routines.

My brother, Rob, at 14, was also a high school student, and he spent his time making soap box cars. These were homemade vehicles, normally built with plywood or fiberglass but with no engine. He would build and race them at the annual soap box car derby. Even though he was not muscular or big, he acted like he was, while wearing his jean jacket and faded blue jeans. He constantly told Jennifer and me that we were ugly dogs. We would both cry to my mother in the hope that she would stop him. When she didn't we would scream at my brother: "Well, you're just a stupid jerk anyway!" He would laugh and walk away. His laughter would hurt us as much as his words.

Twirling batons would later become one of the most stabilizing factors in my life, providing me with a strong social life and confidence. But at the age of nine, it was just for fun. That is, until my first competition, which was at the high school auditorium in Saco, Maine.

Because she was an excellent seamstress, my mother had made our twirling costumes. I was dressed in a sparkly light blue sleeveless leotard with a shiny silver ribbon straight down the front. The costume had rhinestones attached to the ribbon, making it glisten with my movements. Jennifer had a similar costume, but hers was pink and had two shiny ribbons on both sides. I was pleased that they were different. Having anything different to Jennifer was not normal, so my pretty costume was extra special to me.

At the competition our mother stood back to admire us.

"Are you ready to do your routine, honey? Do it just like you did at home," my mother encouraged me. I looked up and saw four judges sitting at a long table. They looked so scary to me. I looked at Jennifer. I saw her rub her hands together and glance behind her, and then at the judges. I got the feeling she was scared too.

"When is Jennifer up?" I asked. In the past, for small shows we would perform a duet where we twirled together, but this time we were performing solos. I had never twirled all by myself and I was worried for both Jennifer and myself.

"Your sister's doing her solo right before you – so you can watch her," my mother added. Good, I thought. I'll see what she does and I'll copy. At that point, a loud voice announced over the speakers: "Set 24 - Lane 3, Novice Beginner Solo, Jennifer Sinclair. I watched Jennifer jump down from the bleachers and take her spot in front of all four judges. I couldn't believe how brave she was.

The recording of the band music, so familiar to us from our practices, started playing. Jennifer saluted the judges, holding the baton in her right hand with it vertical against the left side of her body, then she tossed the baton in the air and caught it. I was mesmerized as I watched her perform her routine. She twirled the baton using just her fingers, horizontally and then vertically. She even did an elbow roll, where she held her left elbow out and rolled the baton over it. The 90 second routine ended with a final toss of the baton, which Jennifer caught before she saluted the judges again. I saw her give one last smile and then she turned around and ran back to where my mother and I were sitting.

My hands were sweaty and my mind was blank.

"Go ahead honey, you need to do your routine now."

My mother lifted my baton from the bleachers and handed it to me as I got up slowly to make my way onto the gymnasium floor. My movements were automatic.

"Hurry honey, the music will be starting," she warned. I picked up my speed slightly and stood in front of the judges.

The voice over the loud speaker announced "Set 25, Lane 3, Novice Beginner Solo, Julia Sinclair." I looked at the judges. I saluted them, and then my mind went totally blank. I couldn't remember any of my routine. I twirled the baton in my right hand and then put it in my left hand and twirled it some more. I looked up at the bleachers at my mother and Jennifer and they seemed so far away. I looked at the judges; two of them looked at me and started writing on their clipboards. I wondered what they were writing. I spoke to myself in my head: "Keep twirling the baton, keep twirling the baton, oh wait, keep smiling……twirl and smile. Twirl and smile…..they judge you on smiling, keep smiling." I moved the baton from hand to hand, twirling. I incorporated no tricks and no baton tosses into the air. After a very long minute and a half, the music ended and I was thankful to be able to salute the judges one more time and exit the floor.

I ran back to Jennifer and my mother, and started crying. "It's okay, honey, we're done, you don't need to do any more," my mother assured me. "We'll just wait for the results of this section and then go home."

I stopped crying eventually as we gathered our things. Going home sounded like a good idea to me, and I didn't want to wait for the results of the competition. However my mother and Jennifer did of course, so we waited. A half hour later, the three of us noticed that the results were posted on the tables near the trophies and medals. We walked over to take a look.

"Jennifer! Look, you came in second!" My mother exclaimed as she pointed to her name on the list of 12 girls. I looked at the list and noticed my name was 11th.

The lady behind the awards table congratulated Jennifer and handed her a small heavy medal, shaped like a star with a blue and white ribbon attached to it. The gold medal had an engraved picture of a baton twirler on it, and I thought it was just beautiful. As Jennifer's smile widened from ear to ear, the tears welled up in my own eyes and I couldn't hold them back.

"Mooooooooommy, I want a medal too," I wailed.

I sobbed uncontrollably, taking big gasps of air. Tears ran down my cheeks and onto my sparkly leotard that I so loved. I wiped my nose with my hand and wiped it off on my costume. "I – I – I want a medal!"

Never had Jennifer received a toy that I had not also received. At my house, there were two of everything: two bicycles, two favorite stuffed animals, two Dr. Seuss books. Two! Not one. Now Jennifer had this medal and I did not.

I saw my mother close her eyes and take a long breath and then we walked out into the parking lot. I only became louder. I bawled like an infant that hadn't been fed, "I – I – I said I want a medal! Jennifer has a medal and I don't!" I noticed the people on the other side of the parking lot look up with concern.

My mother's face became bright red and she held her own head in her hands. "I don't have a medal for you, Julia!"

That made me wail even louder. The ride home was a little over an hour and I wept the entire way. I looked over Jennifer's shoulder as she admired her shiny award. I clearly felt that if I stopped crying, the extent of my pain would not be understood.

As soon as we pulled into the driveway, I saw my father outside shoveling snow off the pathway to the backdoor. The tears started streaming again. "D-D-Daddy, J-Jennifer …..medal……2nd…….11th……." I was so upset I couldn't get words out.

"Dear, dear, dear…..I'm sure it's not that bad. Now what happened? Come tell me about it." His eye brows lifted and I felt his true concern.

"So you would like a medal as well?" he said, after listening to everything that had happened.

"Y-yes" I muttered. He asked Jennifer if he could borrow her medal.

"Let's go make you one then." He instructed me to follow him down to his workshop in the basement. Sniffling, I followed. He searched through his leftover sheets of metal from other projects and carefully selected a large sheet of copper. The metal was solid and it was about the same thickness as Jennifer's medal. It was shiny and polished.

"Now, now…….let's see what we can do here," he said, as he took a pencil from a small tin and held the award against the copper sheet to trace it. He carefully drew an outline around the star, with one of the points touching the edge of the copper sheet. I was fascinated, and I stood about two inches away from my father, watching my new medal being made from scratch.

"Okay honey, you need to stand back a little because I'm going to use this machine to cut it out, and there will be sparks, and I don't want you to get hurt," he explained as he grabbed a pair of plastic safety glasses, put them on, and adjusted the metal sheet into the motorized circular saw. So kind. So calm. So caring. He turned on the saw and immediately the sparks started flying as my father leaned in closer to the blade.

I knew my medal would be perfect! But even more pleasing to me was the fact that my daddy cared so much about me that he would make it his first priority to make me a medal.

I held the medal closely, not only as my reward for my attempt at the baton twirling competition but also tangible evidence of my father's love. In the darkest times I would turn to that medal and remind myself that the man who was screaming and shouting was not my real daddy. My real daddy was the man who cared so much about my feelings to make me a token of my worth. And so began my acceptance of bad treatment, when it was followed by good.

CHAPTER 2
IMITATING VIOLENCE

"Violent behavior is learned, and violence begets violence."

– **Ross Bishop,** AUTHOR, SHAMAN, SPIRITUAL TEACHER AND HEALER

"Where's Daddy? Where's Rob and Brian?" I asked my mother. I knew Jennifer was still sleeping and I had seen Debra dribbling her basketball out in the driveway. It was a Saturday morning and my favorite time of the week, because Saturday morning cartoons were on television. I ran over to turn the TV on, turning the channel dial, looking for Scooby Doo.

"Oh, they'll be back soon honey. Why don't you go pour yourself a bowl of cereal."

"But, where are they?" I asked, as I proceeded to climb onto the kitchen counter to stand up to look through the cupboards. I never got in trouble for climbing like a monkey around the kitchen.

I jumped down off the counter and ran into the dining room and asked her again: "Well, where are they, Mommy?"

"They just went fishing early this morning, they should be home soon...."

"They did? How come Daddy didn't wake me up?"

"Well, you don't like to go fishing, that's for boys," my mother responded, as she sat at her sewing machine, meticulously creating new clothing pieces for us, as well as mending clothing that customers had dropped off at the house.

"It is?" I asked.

It was the first time I can remember hearing that something was specifically for boys. And I didn't like it. Why would Brian, just a year older than me, get to profit from special time with our daddy just because of his sex.

"Why is it just for the boys?"

"Because those are the things they like to do," my mother responded quickly, as if already exhausted by my questions. She looked at me above her glasses and directed me again to get a bowl of cereal.

"Mommy, I want to go fishing too!" I told my mother.

My mother rolled her eyes. "Then, talk to your father about that."

I looked up and saw the station wagon pulling into the driveway. Rob and Brian got out of the car, very excited, and my father proudly brought in a 10-inch long trout. He laid it on the kitchen sink as he prepared to clean it. It smelled like dirty socks in a sewer.

"Look what your brother caught! Ten years old and look what he caught!" My father proudly announced.

I was jealous at the pride in his voice.

"Daddy! How come I couldn't go with you?" I whined, following his every move.

"You were asleep," he told me.

"You could have woken me up!"

I realized he was avoiding the true reason he had left Jennifer and myself behind; and it stung.

"Dear, dear, dear.....why don't you find your sister, and turn on some television."

"Daddy! I want to go fishing too!" I insisted, as I shadowed him out to the car and helped him bring his tackle boxes in, and take them down to the basement. "Yes, honey, another time we can."

I went back to the living room and sat on the couch to watch Scooby Doo. Jennifer joined me as the cartoon was ending.

"Daddy went fishing with Brian and Rob and we couldn't go," I informed her. I knew she was the only one who would truly understand the exclusion.

"Why not?"

"Because we're girls" I answered.

"Because we're girls?"

"Yeah, that's what Mommy said"

Jennifer's face went from perplexed to incensed. Her anger satisfied me. I could always rely on her.

We had so many feelings in common all our lives. As well as sharing our mother's womb we had shared the same crib. Having only one crib was the result of my parents expecting only one baby. Ultrasounds were not performed on normal pregnancies at the time, and so my parents only learned of Jennifer's existence after my birth, when the doctor said: "Keep pushing, there's another baby in there."

My parents had intended to stop having babies after Brian was born. The surprise pregnancy didn't only bring baby number four, but baby number five too. My parents were certainly not prepared, or ready, for such a large family.

"Brian!" Jennifer hollered now. Neither of us heard any response. Jennifer ran from the living room, through the dining room and into the kitchen, where my father was now showing Brian how to clean his fish.

"Brian! Why did you go fishing this morning when Julia and I couldn't?"

"I don't know," Brian responded in a low voice. He was always very submissive when confronted by my sister.

"What do you mean, you don't know?" Jennifer demanded.

"I don't know. Daddy woke me up and asked me if I wanted to go fishing, so I did."

"What about Jennifer and me?" I came up behind Jennifer.

"I don't know." He shrugged his shoulders.

"You should have told him to take us!" I raised my voice.

My father's expression changed. I saw his forehead scrunch up and watched him take a big breath in, as if he was holding back saying something. "Marjie!" he hollered. "These kids need looking after!" And with that, he left us all and headed down the wooden steps into the cellar.

I didn't know why he preferred the cellar. He had a nice recliner chair in the living room, with a TV that was no longer being used by us. His cellar workshop was cold, and completely unfinished. The ceiling was just rafters and the walls were cement. Any items needing to be stored were placed in the basement, including tools, guns, fishing poles, knives, extra jars of paint, kerosene, paint brushes, and many more "workshop" items. But he preferred to hide there. Meanwhile, upstairs, we were not letting Brian off the hook. It was as if he alone was responsible for every slight ever made against the female sex.

"Why, why Brian?" Jennifer was badgering. "Why didn't you wake us?"

This repetitive question, along with Brian's mumbled 'I don't know', continued for 20 minutes until my mother came into the kitchen.

"Kids, kids......finish up with cleaning that fish. Twins, go outside and play until things get cleaned up in here. Brian, are you about done? Why don't you just leave it, your father can finish that up. Yes, you go outside too."

"Jesus Christ Almighty!" I heard my father bark as he came up the cellar stairs. "Do I need to do goddam everything in this house?"

"Walter!" my mother implored. "Just go back downstairs. I'll – I'll just take care of this. Kids, go outside, before you start something."

"Marjie, you are always doing all kinds of shit for these goddam kids. Why don't you make them do one goddam thing for themselves, ah? Gimme this, gimme that, that's all we freakin' hear around here, and you run, run, run to do it all for em', spoiled.....that's what they are, spoiled brats."

Contrary to my mother's wishes, none of us had made it outside yet. I was still full of resentment, and now 'nice Daddy' had turned into the 'mean Daddy' again.

"Daddy! I'm not spoiled and I wanted to go fishing, but you didn't take me!" I hollered.

"Take me here, take me there, gimme this, gimme that, you goddam kids don't appreciate a thing, and all you wanna do is take, take, take!" My father fumed as he took off his black-rimmed military-style glasses. From our many past experiences with 'mean Daddy' I understood this to mean things were about to go from bad to worse. At that point, Brian ran out of the kitchen and went upstairs to the large unheated attic where he, Jennifer and I all slept.

"Brian!" Jennifer yelled as she ran after him, with her long brown braids flying behind her. I ran after both of them. Our mother followed us upstairs.

"Aren't you going to do anything Mommy?" I asked. "Do you think it is right that girls are treated differently to boys? Isn't that wrong?"

But I don't think my mother cared one bit about the division of the sexes, and she wasn't about to stand up for her daughters against her husband and sons.

A few weeks later it happened again. I learned my brothers had been invited to my grandfather's house, to spend the entire day raking up dried leaves from both the front and backyards of his house. This might not sound like something we were desperate to be included in, but there was money involved. Brian, Jennifer and I received an allowance of 25 cents a week. Raking the leaves would earn my brothers $10.00 each. I did not understand why my brother, who wasn't even an entire year older than me, was more capable of raking leaves. All of us children had to shovel the long driveway after snow storms, rake up our own leaves in the fall and clean up piles of mowed grass in the summer. I knew I was capable.

My grandfather on my father's side was six feet tall, with a full head of stark white hair; he had the distinguished look of someone who was intelligent, and indeed he was. He was an engineer by trade, and he was well known in the small town of Oakvale. Unfortunately, he wasn't just known for his skills. Grandfather Sinclair was also known by the local police station for driving his small light blue Ford Pinto while intoxicated. The cops would regularly pull him over after witnessing near misses and discover he was drunk. They would then call my parents to bring him home. There were never any arrests or jail time, as drunk driving was not looked upon seriously at the time.

On this particular day, my mother was spending the morning at her sewing machine as I was dressing up Barbie for her wedding to Ken. My father was hunting for a jacket and work gloves in preparation for the day at Grandfather's. I stopped Barbie and Ken's wedding preparations to let my mother know of my desire to earn money at Grandfather's as well. I ran over to her sewing machine, still holding Barbie in her wedding dress.

"Mommy! Brian told me he's earning $10.00 to go over to Grandfather's house and rake!"

"Well, it'll give him something to do," my mother replied, as she walked away holding a sewing needle and some jeans she was mending for a customer. "Now I need to mend these clothes, so why don't you go outside and find something to do yourselves?"

"I want to go over to Grandfather's and earn ten dollars too!" I exclaimed.

"You weren't invited. So why don't you go and practice your baton routine with your sister, and I'll come watch you in a little bit."

"No! I want to go over Grandfather's!" I repeated. At that point, Jennifer, who had been practicing her baton routine in the basement, ran upstairs to make sure her opinion was known as well.

"I want to go too! If Brian is going, we can too!" Jennifer shouted at my mother.

"Girls, I have a migraine. Would you just go outside and find something to do."

"No!" Jennifer and I both screeched simultaneously.

At that moment, my father came up from the basement, and increased his volume to a decibel even louder than ours. "Why are you freakin' kids always in the way. Go find something worthwhile to do and stop bothering your goddam mother!"

"I want to go over to Grandfather's!" Jennifer reiterated, as tears welled up in her eyes. With all the yelling, chaos and Jennifer crying, I started crying too. My father grabbed a hairbrush off the counter in the dining room and came after both Jennifer and me, at full speed. His hair, which was normally combed over his receding hairline, was flying in every direction and his face was beet red.

"You're not leaving this goddam house with that behavior! You freakin' kids think that you run this household! You think you'll always get your way by crying, crying,

crying.....well, I'll give you something to freakin' cry about!" He swung the hairbrush at me and hit me on my left arm, leaving a large red mark in the shape of the brush. I ran towards the back door to the house and cried even louder: "Daddy, stop it!"

"I'll stop it when you goddam kids decide to stop being pains in the ass!" He lashed out and smacked Jennifer on the back as it was the closest part of her body he could reach, but then he got closer and struck her with his fist in her stomach again. She fell to floor, unable to catch her breath. My father's eyes were filled with rage as he looked around for another weapon, and grabbed a yard stick that was propped up in the corner of the room against the wall. Knowing how much he liked to use this weapon, Jennifer crawled up off the floor and bawled: "I hate you, Daddy, I hate you! I hope you die!" She then spun to my mother: "Mommy! Stop him! He's hitting me! Stop him!"

"I can't take this, I just can't take this......" My mother sobbed. "Just stop it, stop it all of you! Jennifer......don't get him going again!" Then she ran into the bathroom.

My father reached over to hit Jennifer again but she and I ran out of the back door. I curled up in a ball on the porch, and waited. I heard my father, mutter: "Jesus Christ Almighty..." and then I heard his footsteps, as he headed back down to the basement of the house. Once I knew he was not coming after us, I snuck back in to check on my mother. I ran to the bathroom door and tried to open it. It was locked.

"Mommy, Mommy!" I hollered through the door, "Are you alright?"

"Yes, honey, just go away. Let me have some quiet...just stop bothering your father," she whispered through her tears.

"But Mommy, he's yelling at us and we didn't even do anything. I didn't say anything to him. Tell him to stop! Why don't you tell him to stop?"

"I – I – I just can't handle this anymore. Just please leave him alone... g- g- go to your room," She muttered as she tried to catch her breath.

"Mommy! Come out! Why won't you come out of the bathroom?"

I begged my mother to unlock the door. After my begging for what seemed like hours, but was probably only 20 minutes, my mother emerged. She appeared worn out, with dark circles under her eyes and her normal auburn-dyed hair completely disheveled.

"Mommy, are you okay?"

"Yes...I just need to lie down...go find your sister and play outside..." her voice trailed off as she went into the room she shared with Daddy and closed the door.

That was the way of education in our house. My father meted out violence and my mother ran away, too afraid to confront it. We were definitely annoying, as only nine year-olds can be, but opportunities to explain or change an opinion were ignored in favor of swearing and hitting. It was not a good example to set. And we copied it, with Brian as our victim. It was not his fault we were treated differently to him but he got the brunt of it. When he refused to agree we should be included in boys' tasks Jennifer hit him, just as Daddy hit her, and I am ashamed to say I took out my aggression on him too. That was the circle of violence in our household. And I so wished it would stop.

I remember the police arriving once because Jennifer had cut my father's leather belt with a knife, after he told her he was going to send her to the Youth Development Center (YDC), better known in our area as the juvenile jail. My father was as angry as I had ever seen him, resulting in him and my sister struggling on the floor with the knife.

My father held my sister's fist tightly with one hand, so she couldn't let go of the knife, and was hitting her with his other hand while screaming at her. Debra called the police for help. My mother told Debra not to make the call, saying: "What will the neighbors think of us now, seeing a police car in our driveway?"

Surprisingly, neither my father's temper nor my mother's shame deterred Debra.

In my young mind I was confused over whose fault this was. Was it Jennifer's because she had cut the belt? Was it my father's because he had started beating her on the kitchen floor? Or was it my mother's, because she just acted the victim and stood back and cried.

It took only ten minutes for the police to arrive.

"Good evening, officers," my father said as he opened the front door, totally calm now. I could hear one policeman speaking but couldn't make out what he was saying. "Oh yes, yes, come on in. Would you like a cup of coffee, tea?"

There were two officers; a male and a female. "Here, dear, have a seat." My father pulled out a chair for the female officer. The male officer explained that they had received a call from the house about a fight.

"Yes, yes," my father responded. "You understand, I'm sure, these kids, spoiled by their mother all day, are almost impossible by the time I get home at night." He smiled, nodding his head as if willing the cops to do the same. They did. "They just need some discipline."

"We do have children as well, so we do understand that they can be challenging," said the male officer, looking at his partner and then at my father. "We just wanted to stop by and make sure everything was alright."

My father was beaming a smile. Nice Daddy was back, even while Jennifer was still licking her wounds upstairs. I thought it was odd neither officer asked to see her. As I watched my father hand them mugs of tea I wondered where Nice Daddy went when Mean Daddy came forward. They truly were two entirely different people. I hoped the police officers would insist our family get some kind of help; would insist my father see someone for his aggression.

But after about 20 minutes the officers each handed my father a business card, and told him he could give them a call if he needed anything in the future. He walked both officers to the door like old friends who hadn't seen each other in 20 years. They grinned, shook hands and wished each other well. My mother had not uttered a word throughout.

I thought to myself: 'Boy, is Jennifer in trouble now!' But then both of us were in trouble. It was at that moment I realized no one was going to help us navigate this nightmare. We were on our own.

CHAPTER 3
ASKING FOR HELP

"Believe the child, until you prove, without a doubt, otherwise. The first time they tell may be the only time."

– TheMamaBearEffect.org NONPROFIT ORGANIZATION FOR PREVENTION
OF CHILD SEXUAL ABUSE

It would be many years before I understood the scourge of alcoholism, and how it often went hand-in-hand with child abuse. I knew my father drank too much but I did not understand that he was an alcoholic. But I did know the constant shouting and fear was wrong.

At our neighbor's house, I saw my friend's parents treating their children with respect. No one raised their voices. When my siblings and I went swimming at the public swimming pool, the life guards had to tell Jennifer and me not to force Brian under the water. It seemed to us that the behavior standards outside of our home were far higher for everyone, adults and children alike.

Eventually I decided that I would try to get us help.

Jennifer and I had started junior high school where there were guidance counselors. We were told that the guidance counselors would be able to help us with any problems we might be experiencing. It occurred to me that maybe one of these guidance counselors could talk to the other members of my family about our dysfunctional relationships.

Mrs. Mancini seemed like a nice lady. At about 5'8, with pitch-black long hair, she reminded me of Cher. She wore dark eye-liner and large gold earrings. Her friendliness with students made me feel she was open to hearing about anything, even my abnormal family. I hoped that she would understand why my home was so chaotic, and help me to have a family that didn't fight constantly.

I decided to stay after school one day, until no one else was around. I didn't want other junior high kids hearing about my problems. I would take the later bus home. I stood in line in the office area, behind other students needing to turn in permission slips and signed report cards. Finally, it was my turn and I asked for Mrs Mancini.

"Julia?" She smiled at me as she approached me. I suddenly felt nervous. I started perspiring. My hands felt wet and sticky. I wiped the sweat from my palms onto my jeans. I'm telling another adult, I thought. On the one hand, I was happy that I might be helping my family. On the other hand, I was nervous because I knew my mother would accuse me of betrayal, and say I was causing even more trouble than Jennifer.

"Have a seat," Mrs. Mancini said, as she pointed to the gray metal fold out chair next to her desk. I sat down and wiped my hands on my pants again.

"I think I know your family," Mrs. Mancini informed me. "Rob and Debra? Are they your brother and sister?"

"Yep," I answered.

"You look just like them!" She smiled. "How can I help you?"

"Well, my family fights all the time. My mother doesn't know what to do. My father yells and hits us, and my mother gets so upset, and my brother …not Rob…I don't know if you know Brian, but my brother minds my sister, and he minds me too. Jennifer is so mean. She yells all the time, and my mother cries. I don't know what to do."

"What do you do?" she asked, raising her dark eyebrows.

"I try to make my mother feel better. I, I, I am mean to Brian too. Ya know, the police come over to my house."

"What happens when the police come over?" she inquired, looking worried.

"Nothing," I whispered.

I saw Mrs. Mancini writing on a pad of yellow-lined paper. I thought it was a good sign, that she was listening and taking notes.

"How long has your family been fighting like this?" She looked at me with concern.

"I don't know; a long time...years?"

"When it's happening, what makes it get better?" It was easy to answer these questions, given I had lived through it so often.

"It gets better if Daddy and Jennifer stop yelling and my mother stops crying. Sometimes, if my mother is at work, Jennifer and I walk to Oakvale General Store , where she works, to get away from Daddy."

"How far is that?" Mrs. Mancini's eyes widened. She seemed very interested in all the details. I thought she might be more helpful than the police officers.

"A couple of miles maybe?" I shrugged my shoulders so she would know I was estimating.

"And what does your mother do?"

"Well, when she's working, Daddy's not there but she tells us not to fight with him. She doesn't like it when we fight with Daddy. Sometimes, we make her cry at her work too."

"That must be difficult for all of you. Let me take a look at this and for now, just try to stay out of the conflicts and help your parents." She smiled at me as she added: "It'll be okay, darling, it'll be okay." I smiled back as she stood up and opened her door. "Okay, okay, thank you Mrs. Mancini." I gathered my book bag and gave her one final nod, and a smile to convey that I was leaving. I knew she would help and it would indeed be okay.

I left the school that day with high hopes. But as the weeks went by, and then the months, I never heard from Mrs. Mancini, or anyone from the school again. I saw her periodically in the hallways, but she never brought it up to me and I didn't want to bother her another time. I assumed that the adults at the school, where I spent most of my days, were unable to help. I decided I needed to try the police again.

So one evening, after school, I walked to the police department and spoke to the juvenile officer. To this officer I confided even more detail about our life. I told him that Daddy hit Jennifer several days a week, and most recently he hit her for burning the rug in our bedroom when she was trying to heat our freezing room with a hot frying pan! I told him that Jennifer bossed Brian around just as much, and she hit him, and my parents didn't stop it.

I ran home afterwards and told my mother that I was getting help for us. I don't know what I expected her to say. I think I just wanted to give her hope.

But in response, I received a long sigh, along with an exasperated: "Good, good honey. Maybe they can help you out. God knows this thing is out of my hands."

I felt it was a strange reply, even then, like she was abdicating all responsibility for what was happening inside our home. I knew my mother felt helpless, but this confirmed to me that she had no idea how to handle Daddy or us.

But months went by and no one came to help. I never heard from the counselor or the police officer again.

I began to realize that what I thought was wrong, and unfair, was actually perfectly acceptable to the adults. Hitting and punching children was obviously not as unacceptable as I believed. Looking back, this realization played a great part in the formation of my character and what I would come to accept in my own life, later on.

CHAPTER 4
FAMILY COUNSELING

"Sometimes families choose an "Identified Patient" as a scapegoat for their

unresolved issues. If you're a black sheep, it's nothing personal."

– www.lonerwolf.com

Even 40 years later, I don't know what inspired my parents to finally see a family therapist. Had the school counselor or the teacher finally got in touch? Or had they recognized the impact all the screaming and hollering was having on us? Or had my mother finally stood up to my father? If she had, we didn't see it. But Brian, Jennifer and I suddenly found ourselves in Dr. Feldman's office, along with our mother and father, staring at his olive green walls.

I was so relieved and a little excited that we were finally going to get the help we so desperately needed. My heart hoped that a more serene homelife was right around the corner. At the age of 12, I had already decided to write a book about our strange family dynamic and called it 'The Dumb Age' after my mother had called our family fighting dumb. I had asked her to buy me a 200 page notebook, but I of course didn't tell her why, and then I wrote about every fight, every dispute, every parental and sibling reaction. I included quotes from the daily fights and filled up the entire notebook, front and back, by the time they said we were going to see a psychiatrist.

"Please do sit down." Dr. Feldman motioned us all towards a couch and a single chair.

I looked at the beige leather couch. It reminded me of the backseat of my family's station wagon. It appeared lumpy and uncomfortable, but this was okay with me because Dr. Feldman was the man who would finally end the 'Dumb Age'. Notebook in hand, I sat at the end of the couch and tried to melt into the corner. Brian, Jennifer and my mother joined me on the bench-like seat, while my father sat in the chair. It matched the lumpy couch in design and was set perpendicular to the sofa.

I looked around the room, and then at the balding man we had come to see. He looked at us over his wide-rimmed glasses, which appeared too big for his face, glancing at me and then at each one of us in turn. Wearing a plaid brown, yellow, and orange leisure suit with a brown turtle neck shirt, he reminded me of how Daddy looked before he left on business trips. I loved it when Daddy went on business trips for two reasons. Firstly, I knew there would be no fighting in the house at all while he was gone, but secondly, and more significantly to me, was that he would bring home toys for us. As soon as he arrived home, we would gather around him, waiting for him to open up his briefcase like he was Santa Claus opening his big black sack of gifts.

"Now, now look what we have here!" He would sound excited as he pulled out a water globe paper weight of the Golden Gate Bridge, and Mad Lib books. By about the fourth gift in for each of us, he would be handing us a pen from the hotel room and we knew the gifts were coming to an end.

How did we end up here? I asked myself, as we sat in that room. Daddy's a nice daddy! Maybe all of this was Jennifer's fault really. She was really mean to Brian and she even got me to be mean to Brian! But then I thought about the force with which Daddy would hit Jennifer, and his bad language, and how he would cuss at us for hardly any reason. Something in our family was broken, and it wasn't just Jennifer.

"Marjie, Walter." Dr. Feldman nodded towards my mother and then my father. He told them he had been working with families in our area for more than nine years. "I'm interested in hearing about what brings you here. But first, I would like to learn each of your names and maybe hear a little bit about each of you." He looked at me first.

"I'm Julia. I'm in 7th grade in junior high. I wrote this book and I like writing," I told him.

"Ah – I see. That's a lot of writing. And how about your sister and brother?" he looked at Brian.

"Brian," was all my brother added, as his overgrown straight bangs fell into eyes. He stared at the shaggy rug beneath our feet.

"Brian" the doctor repeated. "Okay."

Dr. Feldman then looked at Jennifer, next to Brian. Her two pony tails with blue ribbons on each side of her head did not make her look like the "bad seed" that I knew my parents felt she was at this point. "And you?"

"Jennifer.....I go to junior high too." Although she didn't say much she stared back at the doctor with a bravery I didn't feel. She was always braver than the rest of us.

"Well, I guess I'd like to hear what the issues are." Dr. Feldman held his own pad of paper, which was much thinner than my notebook. He wheeled his chair away from his desk to come closer to us.

My father looked quite professional as well, in a light blue blazer. "Well, doctor, it seems there's been quite a lot of disruption in the house these days."

"Disruption?"

"Yes, these kids just don't seem to want to behave, regardless of what we do for them.....they are carted around everywhere, the twins to their baton-twirling lessons, their friends' houses, and Brian has joined his older brother recently at the Civil Air Patrol meetings and nothing we do is enough."

"And why isn't it enough?"

"They just yell and scream and fight and their mother and I are just getting real tired of it." Daddy shook his head as he blinked his eyes.

"I see, and Marjie?"

My mother held the bridge of her nose and closed her eyes. "I just don't know what to do anymore, I just don't know. When I was a kid, children were supposed to be seen and not heard, but these girls--they are just cut from a different piece of cloth. Their older sister, who goes to the university now, never gave us problems like this."

I stared at my mother, incredulous. She was actually blaming us.

"How about your other son?" the doctor asked.

"Nope – he does his own thing..." my mother's voice faded off.

"He calls me ugly!" Jennifer added.

"See, it's stuff like that, interrupting - no respect at all." My father glared at Jennifer.

"Well he does, he calls me and Julia ugly dogs and you don't do anything about it!" She was staring at our mother now.

My father took the opportunity to explain to Dr. Feldman just how badly behaved Jennifer was. "Doctor, I don't know if you've seen kids like this before: loud, rude, interrupting, constantly causing so much fighting - she even took out a knife on me last month! What do you do with these types of problem children? What about the Youth Development Center? Marjie and I are just at our wits end with all of this. Marjie has migraines every day and these kids just rule the household."

"I see." Dr. Feldman contemplated. "And Julia, what do you see as being the issue? I see your book is called 'The Dumb Age.' What does that mean?"

"Well, there's so many fights in our house, every single day, and Daddy asks Rob and Brian to go fishing with him and canoeing but we don't get to go. So, Jennifer bosses Brian around and Brian will do anything she says."

"Anything eh?" The doctor confirmed with me.

"Yup," I replied.

"What if your parents or I told him to do something else? Would he do that instead of doing what Jennifer tells him to do?"

"Nope," I answered. "He will always do what Jennifer tells him to do."

"I don't think that's the case." Dr. Feldman tilted his head down and looked over the top of his glasses at me.

"He will do what Jennifer says," I reiterated.

"If I told Brian to leave this office right now, he will, regardless of what your sister says."

"Not if Jennifer tells him to stay," I shook my head.

Dr. Feldman looked at Brian and then at Jennifer. Brian continued to look at the floor and Jennifer returned the doctor's glare. She was definitely challenging him.

"Brian, please leave my office," Dr. Feldman nodded at Brian. Brian looked up with a resigned look, stood up, and walked to the door. His hand hadn't reached the door knob yet when Jennifer intervened,

"Brian, sit back down."

Brian walked slowly back to the couch and sat down.

"Brian, I said to please leave my office," Dr. Feldman repeated.

Again, Brian stood up and got as far as he did in his prior attempt.

"Sit down, Brian," Jennifer said staring at him with the same glare that my father would use on her, before hitting her.

Brian sat back down immediately.

"Get up and leave the office now." The doctor's face was now turning a shade of pink that reminded me of Daddy's face prior to a fight.

Not giving Brian any time to even move towards the door, Jennifer commanded: "Sit down." She had shortened the phrase. Brian did so again.

"Get up," the doctor instructed with his own shortened phrase. Brian stood up submissively.

This continued for 10 minutes, as Brian went back and forth, sitting and standing, as if it was a training exercise. My parents and I just stared at the scene. I was thinking that at least the doctor would see a good example of the control Jennifer had over Brian, but I couldn't see how it was doing anything to show my father how wrong he was to physically abuse his children.

The doctor finally decided to change the strategy.

"This is my office and I will say what happens in my office, Jennifer. You leave my office," he instructed, as his face turned a much darker shade of pink.

"Then Brian is coming with me," she demanded.

"Not if I say he's not." The doctor's ears were now matching the color tone of his face.

"Brian – come with me," Jennifer directed, as she stood up herself. This time Brian got up to leave at Jennifer's command.

"Brian is staying, you are leaving! Brian, you sit down!"

"Brian, come with me!" Jennifer contradicted the doctor's demand.

As this apparent power struggle continued between Jennifer and the doctor, Brian said absolutely nothing and simply followed the instruction of the last demand, regardless of the mouth from which it came. This repetition lasted much less time and within two minutes the doctor picked up all 85 pounds of Jennifer, opened his door, and placed her screeching and shaking body in the hallway of the counseling center.

"Brian!" she screeched from the other side of the door. "You come out here now!"

The doctor stared at Brian and said: "You are not going anywhere. You are staying right in that seat." Brian obeyed the doctor.

"Brian, Brian!" she continued shrieking. Jennifer was shouting at the top of her lungs.

The doctor then demanded she leave the building. She refused. At this point, he left his office for a few minutes and all I heard was continued shrieking and crying in the distance. He returned a few minutes later. Even from inside the building, I could still hear the screeching coming from outside. Part of me thought: 'Just another day, just another fight.' But another part of me continued to hold out hope that this man would know what he was doing and would help my family. Maybe he was just starting with Jennifer and then would move on to my parents. Surely he could see how badly it was affecting Jennifer.

"Let's talk about this on the phone. We are at the end of the hour," was all the doctor added when he came back in. He let out a sigh and straightened out his jacket as he too, like the police officers a couple of months earlier, handed my father a business card.

Was it his card, I thought? Or was it a card to the YDC? Maybe he agrees with my father, that the juvenile jail is the only place that can handle Jennifer.

My parents, Brian and I got into the car, as Jennifer huddled against the side of the brick building and cried. My father demanded that she get in the car, but she refused. Eventually, as the sun went down and the day turned into night, we went home without her.

None of this surprised me anymore. We had been through so many nightly fights, so many bike rides and "run-away" walks, both day and night, to escape the violence, that leaving my sister downtown huddled against the side of a building was not at all out of the ordinary.

Later that night I heard the car start up, and watched my mother back it out of the driveway. About 20 minutes later, both Jennifer and my mother came home with tears in their eyes. I didn't ask what further discussion had occurred. I didn't ask my parents what the therapist was going to do to help, or even if we were going back. After about a month, I just assumed we were not returning.

My 12 year-old mind was putting the pieces together. My parents couldn't handle my family, and they certainly could not handle Jennifer. The police couldn't help us, the school counselor couldn't help us and now the therapist couldn't help us. The only hope for me and for my siblings was to grow older and spend less and less time at home until we could all go to college.

I signed up for school-related trips, group camp outs laid on by outside organizations, and later, much longer programs like Upward Bound, a federally-funded college preparation program for at-risk youth. My plan was to stick around when Daddy was nice, and leave when Daddy got mean. And both were sure to happen.

In the ensuing years, both did happen. The family fights continued and the reasons were just as unpredictable as they had been in my younger years. My father would sometimes go into a rage for simple things like my eating the last of the ice cream in the freezer, my knocking over a pile of canned goods by accident, or anyone having the television up too loud. Other times, Daddy patiently helped me with my homework, took me on peaceful hiking trips and taught me how to drive, while diligently saving money to send me and all my siblings to college. My mother took me to baton twirling competitions all over New England and handmade my costumes and clothing. She, later, worked full time to make sure we could go to college as well. The love of both of my parents was clear. But so was their instability.

I learned from my daddy that it was okay for men to be mean and vengeful and treat women with complete disrespect. I learned from my mother that violence from a husband to his wife, and to his children, was acceptable. I also learned that my mother felt that it was a woman's duty to stay with her man, no matter what, helped perhaps by the fact that the next day the nastiness could change to sweetness. If you waited long enough, things would change. But, I never learned what "long enough" was. Once, when my brother Rob was being repetitively mean and disrespectful to me, I asked my mother how many chances I should give him before deciding not to have any relationship with him at all, and her answer was "as many as it takes." So I knew, that in order to be accepted by my mother, there was no limit to the chances that you should give people, especially the people that society deemed we should love for a lifetime.

To my mother, marriage definitely meant forever, and there was never a good reason to leave. It would be years before I realized that I was being conditioned to choose my future husband.

SECTION 2
YOUNG ADULTHOOD

CHAPTER 5
FALLING IN LOVE

"People whom are addicted to drama will tend to fall for those whom will give them drama, despite how painful it can be."

– **WhisperText LLC**, IOS AND ANDROID MOBILE APP, ANONYMOUS

Approaching young adulthood, with me, the nice guys finished last. I just had no chemistry with the sweet ones. I was attracted to the dark and brooding. That was certainly how I ended up in bed with Randy Castleton. Let me clarify, this was a bed in the house that he shared with his girlfriend. Although, those circumstances should probably have been an indicator to me that this was not the type of man I should date, that thought never occurred to me at the time.

At 23 years old, having just come out of a relationship with a person who was addicted to his work, I was falling in love again. This man not only made me a priority over his work schedule, but also over his current girlfriend! This just made my heart melt. As I lay on top of the bed with him, knowing that we would soon make love for the first time, I admired how his brown hair matched the color of his eyes, and his dark complexion, and I felt like the luckiest person alive.

I had met Randy a few months prior to this, while at my first real job out of college, at a community health center, but we were both dating other people. Since my work-addicted boyfriend had broken up with me a month earlier, I had been heartbroken. My friends were getting engaged, getting married, and I was single again. Being single was not acceptable to me. Like my friends, I wanted to be picking out bridesmaids dresses, venues and wedding cakes, but now I was starting from scratch again. Randy and I had already gone out for drinks, runs, and shared many conversations that showed me what a deep thinker he was. We discussed subjects like whether or not fate exists; God; prior relationship mistakes, and each of our dreams for our lives. I had been trying to convince myself that just being friends with this guy would be fine, since he had already told me he was in a six year relationship. But the truth was, I was hoping to end up in just the spot I found myself in at that moment.

I looked at his biceps and how the curvature of his muscles blended into his shoulders, and formed a build that I had only seen on men at the gym. I melted even more when he started kissing my neck. I did try to put up some defense at the last minute, but in my head the deed was already done. The words that I uttered contradicted the physical feelings racing through me.

"Randy, this isn't right. It is unethical, immoral and wrong. You have a girlfriend." As if he needed the reminder, but I was voicing my own conflicts.

"I'm not married!" he whispered back, smiling, as he moved the kisses over to my mouth.

I waited for a break in the kissing. "Your girlfriend is so lucky.....to have you all the time."

"Well, she doesn't take advantage of having me in bed," he smirked, right before turning the pecks into French kisses. I quickly forgot about his girlfriend as we consummated the affair. I was completely hooked; physically and emotionally.

I had it all. What more could a girl want? I had found all the qualities I desired in one person; deep, loving, good-looking, sweet in bed, formally educated, hard-working.......but wait, I didn't have him. He had a girlfriend. Someone else had him. I had to remind myself of that.

At the time, I still respected and loved that Randy seemed to be opening up his soul to me. He explained that he wasn't in love with his girlfriend, but he just didn't have the heart to break up with her. Having been told the same thing by my ex-boyfriend, that he had been seeing someone else and just "hadn't had the heart" to break up with me, I felt sadness for the entire situation, and especially for Randy's girlfriend. I didn't want anyone to feel as broken-hearted as I had been. However, I did feel the splitting up was going to occur anyway and I wanted to start planning my future with my soon-to-be new boyfriend and maybe someday husband.

Thus, the honeymoon period of our relationship began even before the ending of Randy's current relationship. We went out for dinners and drinks, sang at Karaoke bars, worked out at the gym, ran in road races and continued having passionate sex as part of our normal routine. I loved being adored by him. It had only been a couple months, but he claimed that I was everything he ever wanted. I already knew he was everything that I ever wanted. Certainly, my boring, workaholic ex-boyfriend hadn't been anywhere near as obsessed with me as Randy was. Two months into that relationship, my ex-boyfriend and I had just been getting to know each other. This, on the other hand, was true love.

I knew Randy just needed to put his girlfriend behind him to have the life he really wanted, with me. It did not occur to me that I might be becoming his next victim, one in a long line of women. That did not match my romantic daydreams at all, and denial of reality was something I was getting very good at.

When I wasn't with him, I went out with my friends, worked at my entry level job to make ends meet, lived with other girlfriends, and wished I was with him. I imagined how when we were finally together, I wouldn't have to share housing with roommates; we could combine our money and expenses and it would be so much easier. Life would be the dream that it should be, with the perfect man.

And it was while I was cuddling with that perfect man, some months later, that he told me he loved me. We were enjoying one of our many lunches together in his office, as I sat on his lap, giving him as many kisses and hugs as I could.

"I was thinking about something the other night...and I want to tell you," he whispered into my ear.

"Oh yeah? What's that?" I smiled, as I leaned back and looked at him.

"I love you," he declared, his eyes meeting mine.

The smile I already had increased in size as I returned his sentiment.

"I love you too. I just didn't say it to you because I didn't want to scare you," I whispered back.

The whispering wasn't so much romantic, as an attempt to make sure the rest of the building didn't hear our conversation through the thin walls of his office. It didn't help that my voice had a tendency to be louder than it should be most of the time, no doubt due to my childhood, to the point that someone who was deaf could probably feel the vibration of my voice through surrounding furniture.

"Scare me?" he questioned. "That doesn't scare me at all. I'm 32, not 22. I'm not afraid of love."

How refreshing, I thought. So unlike all the guys my age! Randy was mature, and ready for real love.

It wouldn't be until years later that I put the pieces together, and recognized his insecurity; realizing that he had wanted to be sure I loved him before disposing of his current girlfriend. He wasn't afraid of love; he was actually overly afraid of not having love.

"So, I broke up with Lindsey, ya know..." He looked at me with a half-smile referring to his girlfriend now by name .

"You did? What happened. How is she taking it?" I knew their break-up would be difficult because they still owned a house together.

"Well – sometimes she's fine and sometimes, it's like she doesn't understand. She asked me this morning if I wanted to get into the shower with her...."

"She's trying to get you back!" I blurted out loudly as I suddenly converted into the jealous girlfriend.

Rather than being jealous, I should have been asking myself why I was dating someone who wasn't single, still living with a significant other, and telling me all about their private conversations. It didn't occur to me to see it as a snapshot of his character, or more importantly, a snapshot of my own character and my own immature vision of "love".

Eventually Randy's girlfriend did move out, going back to New Jersey. It immediately changed the basis of our relationship. For many months, I had been living as a single person. I had both female and male friends and we went on trips. I was part of a pen pal program for soldiers at war, and I didn't hide it from Randy. But as we both lay on his living room floor one afternoon, having finished watching a movie, I found out that Randy had other expectations of me. I had excitedly told him about a trip one of my good friends, Nickie, and I were planning when I noticed the shift in his mood.

"You know, Julia, I don't understand. Why would you want to fly to Florida with your friend Nickie! You know how uncomfortable that makes me!"

Nickie and I had been friends since our first day working together at the community health center, and although we came from different backgrounds, we got along well and shared in each other's happiness and heartbreaks.

"What's wrong with me going on vacation with a friend?" I asked Randy.

He scowled and wrinkled his forehead.

"Anything could happen you know. What if someone tries to pick you up? You think I'm okay with that?" He raised his voice slightly.

"No one's going to try to pick me up and even if they do, don't you think I'm old enough to handle that? I am an adult - you know. I'm perfectly capable of handling those types of situations." I sighed and rolled my eyes hoping that he would understand how ridiculous he sounded.

"Well, you're only 23, and when I was 23, I was interested in…" He shook his head. "Well, it doesn't matter. I just don't like it. And then in May, you're going to Outward Bound. I never had to deal with this with Lindsey. She was happy being with just me, and... and….you…you even want to visit a male friend when in Colorado while you're out there!"

"I've been friends, just friends, with many men for years. I'm not going to drop my friendships!" I raised my voice too, wanting him to know where I stood on the issue.

I had seen my girlfriends go out with men in the past who had got upset at them for something as simple as hugging an old college friend at the grocery store. My girlfriends had literally changed their personalities in order to try to make their boyfriend feel more secure in the relationship. In my mind, hell would freeze over before I was controlled by someone like that. Being an outgoing person, friends both female and male always received a warm welcome from me and this wasn't going to change. I was crazy about Randy, but I was determined to remain myself as well as have this relationship in my life.

In February, I jumped on a flight with Nickie to Florida for a week of sunshine. Being able to escape the New Hampshire winters was something new to me, as my prior life was full of college exams and writing papers, which combined to create a lack of time as well as a lack of funds for anything beyond living expenses. As long distance telephoning was expensive I devised an innovative way to make Randy feel loved while I was gone. I wrote him a series of love letters and left them out on my dining table in my apartment. I also left him a message on his answering machine letting him know that the letters were waiting for him to pick up. I wanted him to understand and know that even though I was a thousand miles away, I was completely in love with him.

I had also provided Randy with the phone number of Nickie's mother's house, since we were staying there the whole week.

He called the next day while Nickie and I were at the beach. I ran across the eat-in kitchen on our return, holding my AT&T calling card so I could call him long distance and use the precious minutes to tell him how much I missed him.

"Hi Randy!" I shouted happily as soon as he picked up his phone. I did not expect the angry voice I heard in return. He sounded like my father when he was drunk. This was a Randy I had never heard before. I was shocked at his volume, at his tone, and the pure nastiness of the words that came out of his mouth.

"I went to your apartment, and I went through everything!"

"What are you talking about?"

"I went through everything and you know what I found?"

I could feel the vibration of his angry voice through the telephone.

I couldn't understand. He had gone through everything in my apartment? Why would he do that, I thought?

"Do you know what I found?" He was screaming now into the phone.

"No, I don't....I told you where your letters were, did you see them?"

"I don't care about the letters you wrote to me! I went through everything in your apartment and I found the letters from Juan!"

Juan was my friend from the pen pal program. In his letters he seemed like a typical guy in his 20s. We exchanged letters and tidbits about our lives.

"Yes Randy, I have been writing to him since the summer. You knew that. Why did you go through my stuff? What were you looking for?"

"You told him about your tattoo!" he growled.

"Yes, I just got the tattoo. I tell everyone about it!" I was angry now at his tone, and what he had done, so I raised my voice in return.

"He's flirting with you! You shouldn't be writing to him!" His voice was the loudest I had ever heard. He was gasping for breath after every third word. He sounded like he was having a panic attack, such was his frenzy.

"I'm sure the guy flirts with lots of people. I just signed up to write letters. I'm not going to stop just because you don't like it!" The feeling of having someone trying to control me infuriated me. My mind bounced back to being a child, and having to defend myself against a grown man who was constantly blowing up at me for trivial reasons.

"You're damn right I don't like it, and if you want to do that, if you want to do that – fine, then there is no more us!" I heard another gasp for breath and then a click as he hung up on me.

I sat down slowly at the kitchen table in a state of shock. Nickie looked over at me from across the room with her mouth open. From the expression on her face, which I had seen so many times before, I knew what she was thinking, and what she was about to say. It was, what the hell just happened? I didn't even wait for her to ask. I broke down in tears and between anger and sadness told Nickie about the whole conversation.

"He's a nut case, Julia. He's Borderline."

Nickie and I worked with very low functioning mentally ill people at the community health center and that was my only experience with what "Borderline" meant. I thought of the patient we had worked with who needed assistance with everything, including food shopping, taking medications, and all daily life skills.

"Nickie! Why do you say that. He's not that bad. I love Randy!"

"He's just so freakin' dramatic, just like the Borderlines at the community health center." She shook her head at my inability to see him the same way.

I felt so confused; heartbroken and angry all at the same time. I adored this man, how could he not trust me? How could he go through all my things? How could he blow up at me when he was the one hadn't respected my privacy.

I took a deep breath. I decided I would handle this in a mature fashion. I thought about how much I loved him and that I would do anything to get our relationship through this stumbling block. My mother and father had been married for 32 years at this point, and they had had unreasonable screaming matches involving hysterics and crying, and they were still together so maybe this wasn't out of the ordinary.

I thought about solutions, maybe some counseling to convince him how much I loved him. I thought about how much pain he must be in without my being there to reassure him. A sad cloud enveloped me, like an aura around my whole being. Like my mother, whose primary concern was to make the yelling stop and to not upset my father, I too wanted the fight to end and for Randy to no longer be upset. I didn't have to wait long.

After a sleepless night for me , and a sadness that it was ruining the holiday, he called the next day and was a completely different person. He was not angry or shouting, but in tears.

"I'm not going to give you an ultimatum," he assured me. I started crying immediately upon hearing his cracking voice.

"What about yesterday? What about 'No Us' if I didn't do what you wanted?"

"I – I don't know…you don't know my background, Julia…my childhood was not a happy one. I felt abandoned, unloved, and unable to trust those who loved me. Without realizing it, I've spent years running from this. I'm not running anymore. I'm not going anywhere. I want to be with you for the rest of my life….would you be willing to go to counseling with me to work on our issues?"

My heart swelled. "Sure, I will!" I wiped the tears from my face. I was so thrilled that he had thought of counseling too. Nickie handed me a tissue as she urged me to finish up the call by moving her hand in a circular motion quickly and pointing to the door. She then lifted her head back with her hand in front of her face, making believe she was drinking a beer to remind me of our plans to attend a party on the beach that night.

"Ok, Randy, I need to go….but I love you," I sighed, happy that everything was working out so well.

"I love you too, don't worry, we'll get through this and I appreciate how forgiving you are! And thank you!" He squeezed in words of gratitude for having me in his life. As Nickie and I headed to the beach, there was no way I would even look at another guy. I knew inside that I had the sweetest man on earth.

CHAPTER 6
A WAR ZONE TURNS INTO A PROMISE FOR LIFE

"Smart Women Know the difference between being in love and being in pain"

– Steven Carter and Julia Sokol, AUTHORS OF WHAT SMART WOMEN KNOW

Upon arriving back from vacation, a dozen red roses from Randy were waiting for me at my apartment. My heart filled with joy. This was real love, I thought. Randy hadn't left me, and like my father and mother, I knew now that he would always come back, regardless of the prior conflict. We were just getting acquainted; adjusting to a new relationship.

Two months later there was another test. I returned from taking the Certified Public Accountant (CPA) exam for the third time to find what appeared to be an accounting snow storm in my bedroom. Wrinkled and torn up papers, class notes and textbook pages were strewn all across the bed and on the floor. I found a card from my friend Michael in the middle of the chaos, ripped in half.

"What the hell?" I exclaimed out loud to myself, before wading through the paper to the phone on the wall. As I dialed Randy's number, I could also see some letters from Juan in the melee.

He picked up on the second ring. I didn't give him even a second to say hello.

"What the hell is your problem?" I hollered.

"My problem? You have the problem!" he retorted. "You shouldn't be writing to male friends. They use the word 'Love' at the end of their letters. I'll bet you just eat that up!"

I felt his intense anger and hostility through the phone line.

"You mean Michael? Michael is like a brother to me! I have no idea why you are like this, and why you are so convinced that I am looking to cheat on you. And you think it is okay to break into my house to find out!"

"You made me do that!" He interrupted me. "You are the one with the issues, Julia! I have my own theories, and I know you'll hate it, but my theory is that you came from a very dysfunctional family and you have boundary and control issues."

"Really? And you are my therapist now?" I added sarcasm to my anger.

"You did not get a lot of emotional support or attention from home, so you overcompensate through having many friends! How does that manifest itself, Julia?" Without giving me a chance to respond, he proceeded to answer his own question. "You have yet to have a serious, long-term, mature relationship. Your last relationship was with a guy who clearly had as many problems with being close as you do! So he avoided you, and that's why you have to have friends!" He stopped to take a breath so I took the opportunity to fire back.

"So glad you got that all figured out for me, Randy! Save it for your mentally ill clients. I have friends because it is normal to have friends, and I happen to be an extrovert! Much to your obvious dislike, I don't exclude friends based on their sex!"

I looked up to see my housemate gesturing at me to lower my voice. I mouthed the word 'sorry' as I pointed to the phone receiver and made a cuckoo sign, twirling my finger in a circle by my head. As if he actually saw it, Randy's voice bellowed down the phone line.

"That's it. We are broken up! You know, I never could understand your priorities. I can't believe you gave up on this great relationship with me just for your friends. I was the best guy that you will ever find and now you have ruined our relationship. I was loving; I always put you first; I was motivated and educated and we had great sex."

I countered: "Are you done, Randy? Listen to yourself! You are so full of yourself, Randy. You are arrogant and childish."

I was so sick of his invading my privacy, accusing me of acts that existed only in his mind, and never recognizing how completely inappropriate his actions were, always rationalizing them.

"I wouldn't have gone through your stuff if you didn't give me reason to. You aren't like Lindsey. I could always trust Lindsey. She made me feel safe."

I didn't point out the obvious; that he had left Lindsey. But I did point out that he was still in contact with his ex. They were communicating to sell their house but I had also found friendship cards from her that he had left out in his kitchen.

"What I don't understand is that I am not allowed to have regular friends, but you are allowed to carry on seeing Lindsey." The jealous girlfriend inside me rose to the fore.

"I need to call Lindsey for support when we are fighting!"

"You need to call your ex-girlfriend for support. Are you kidding me?" I shouted. Why couldn't he see his double standard? It infuriated me even further.

He decided to end the call with one last statement. "You just need to grow up and understand what a real relationship is!" Then click, he hung up on me. I had no desire to call him back.

For the next two days we did not speak. It seemed like every hour that went by, a deeper sadness entered my body. I had no desire to eat or go out with friends. They were already wondering what I saw in Randy. I was determined not to be the one to call him. I wanted him to call me and apologize. It was while I was on the phone with my sister that I heard the call waiting beeps.

"Jennifer! I gotta go. I think Randy is beeping in!" I happily picked up the other call and was thrilled when I heard Randy's calm and peaceful voice.

"Hi Sweetie"

I smiled and let out a sigh of relief. I knew instantly that we were back together.

"Listen," he continued. "I shouldn't have gone through your things. I'm sorry. I don't want to fight with you. I just love you so much that I can't help myself sometimes. I just couldn't help myself."

"I don't do that to you," I countered, in a soft voice to make sure he knew I wanted to get along as well. I heard him inhale as he continued his plea.

"I know, I know. And I promise I won't do anything like that ever again. Ever! I love you and I want you in my life forever!" There was a silent pause and then: "How about you come over tonight and we'll rent a movie and I'll make us dinner?"

"Sure!" I was ecstatic that the fight was over. I agreed to bring over some Ben and Jerry's ice-cream, to celebrate our getting back together and getting over the latest hurdle.

As the months turned into a couple of years, these types of struggles continued regularly but we would always make up within a day after the argument. I told myself that these types of fights were bound to happen in long-term relationships. The fact that we always got back together meant that it was real love, just like my parents.

There was the fight when we were signing up for massage therapists. He said that he could never go to a male massage therapist because, being heterosexual, he didn't like the idea of a man's hands touching him. I told him I agreed and said I would prefer a man rather than a woman. I reached for the phone to schedule our appointments but he took it from me and hung up, demanding that I see a female massage therapist.

"I thought we both agreed that we would get massages from the opposite sex?"

"No, we are both seeing female massage therapists. I don't want some strange guy touching you."

We never went.

Another time, a fight broke out between us as a result of my hunting around the house for my running bra. Randy was on the phone and my housemate was emptying my stuff from the dryer. While talking on the phone, I hollered to her:

"Where's my running bra! I need it for this afternoon!"

A male friend was in the dining room, waiting for one of my housemates. The guy waiting for my housemate jokingly commented: "What problems you girls have!" Randy was on the phone and heard it.

"You tell him to mind his own business!" he said.

"He has not done anything," I laughed.

"You tell him!" He screamed back.

These types of screaming matches, along with his continuation of his friendship with his ex-girlfriend, which did bother me, turned our relationship into scenes worthy of reality television. But I still felt it was normal and just a series of hiccups.

The fights were interspersed with good times; going out for food and drinks, seeing his friends that were slowly becoming our friends; watching movies and talking about how wonderful our future married life would be together. But I was noticing a trend. These fights would erupt whenever I was not around Randy. If I was away, it seemed like he would do something to create a drama.

I decided we needed to finally set up the appointment to see a therapist like we had discussed. Surprisingly, Randy still agreed to join me. We both told her how we each felt. I explained my upset about his secret communications with his ex-girlfriend. Randy brought up my desire to have both male and female friends. When the therapist said that she felt having friends of both sexes was appropriate, but secret keeping was not, Randy stared at her with empty, cold eyes and got out of his chair.

"You have no idea what you are talking about! I am not wasting any more of my time with you. I know what I need: you do not."

He left the office, slamming the door on his way out.

We both sat there for a minute. I grabbed a tissue and wiped away the tears rolling down my cheeks.

"See. How can I change that? He doesn't care."

"Julia, that may very well be exactly who he is. That is him. Now, you just have to decide if that's what you want."

I took a deep breath and closed my eyes. I told myself that I knew Randy better than the therapist. I knew Randy better than Lindsey. I knew Randy better than anybody. He wasn't really the way he seemed. And besides, that little part about him, whatever it was that we just saw, he would be able to change that. I told myself that he would change because he loved me so much. I just knew it.

As time went on, I began to interpret Randy's inability to let go of his prior relationship as the real issue in our relationship. If we could just get rid of Lindsey, our relationship would be everything we dreamed about. I saw Lindsey as my competition for Randy's love and come hell or high water, I was going to win him.

After the session with the therapist the intensity of the arguments decreased. I felt this was a breakthrough, however looking back, I realize this was probably because we were spending every free minute together, and there was no reason for him to become jealous. But at the time we concluded that we had made it through the rough patch and the hard times were now behind us. We discussed how well we were doing and considered that we may even be ready to get married. I noted that a lot of people got married after dating for about two years, so it seemed as if the timing might be right. One of my aunts had got married after only a month, and she was still married 50 years later. I knew I wanted Randy, and I wanted to get married, so it was a perfect fit. And Randy seemed keen too, although he didn't ask me to marry him.

A week later, we were out walking on a wooded trail when Randy asked if I wanted to go to a seafood restaurant nearby.

"Are you sure?" I asked him, well aware how expensive it was.

"Yes!" He said. "We haven't had seafood in a while!" I didn't argue. Sometimes Randy was impulsive.

"Table for two. Castleton." He smiled at the waitress. I wondered why he stated his name.

The waitress led us to what was clearly the best table in the restaurant. We sat looking over a beautiful waterfall, surrounded by overarching pine trees; a scene that could have been right out of National Geographic. I was admiring the view but Randy was pulling something out of his pocket. He opened a little black box and asked: "Will you marry me?"

It was so romantic. Tears of happiness rolled down my cheeks. "Yes, of course!" I took the ring and put it on my left ring finger, not even waiting to give him the chance to do it as I was so excited. "Wow, it's beautiful!" I reached out my arm and looked at how the ring sparkled on my hand.

"It's the diamond my mother had. It's a family heirloom," Randy explained. "I had it reset into this ring." He smiled and explained that he had made reservations at this restaurant specifically, and had planned this moment for weeks. The waitress brought over a mini-cake with lovely red and pink frosting roses adorning it.

"Congratulations," she said as she set it down in front of me.

"And this too!"

"Yes. I planned it all," Randy confirmed, smiling at the pleasure it was giving me. I was thrilled by all the thought he had put into this special proposal. I excused myself for a few minutes, ran out to the car and called my mother. I cried, she cried. Later that evening, when at home, I called every single friend I had. "I'm getting married!" I shrieked to each of them. Most of them congratulated me, asking when the big day would be. I decided to ignore the slight hesitation in my friend, Nickie's voice, as she wished me the best. "So, you guys worked everything out? Great Julia…that's really great."

My dreams were coming true and that is what I wanted to focus on .

With a fiancé and an engagement ring, I could now definitely start the wedding planning officially. The next day I went to see my parents to show off my ring and they offered to provide money to cover some of the wedding costs. I gladly accepted, because I was determined to make this the nicest wedding my family had ever been to. My mother and I sat together in her sewing room, surrounded by thread spools of every color and canisters of extra buttons.

'Julia, what do you think of wearing my wedding dress?" she asked. It was a classic traditional wedding dress, fitted at the bodice, with a small waistline leading out to a full skirt. The neckline and sleeves were sheer lace. I had grown up seeing the dress in a black and white photo hanging on my parents' bedroom wall. I loved the idea.

"Is it still white? What about a veil?" I pictured myself, walking down the aisle just like my parents had 35 years before.

"Yes, it is and what about a hat. You could wear a hat like Princess Diana's hats!" My mother spoke quickly as the ideas streamed in her head. I would be the first in my family to get married. "And what do you think about inviting Madelynn, the woman who made me the dress!"

"Sure! That would be awesome!"

Madelynn was around 80 years old and she would get to see the dress worn again by the next generation. This would make the celebration even more meaningful.

"I could do all the fittings and make the dress perfect for you. This will be so nice!" My mother smiled and looked at me as if evaluating how well the dress would fit. My mother had been really thin in her twenties, and I had a similar build.

The next few months were filled with wedding dress fittings, ordering invitations, looking at venues, tasting cakes and selecting the bridesmaids and groomsmen. After being in a number of weddings as a bridesmaid, I was so excited to finally be the bride.

CHAPTER 7
A FAIRY-TALE WEDDING

"All women marry their father. They marry who their father was. They marry who they wanted their father to be, or they marry their fantasy about their father."

– Iyanla Vanzant, AMERICAN NEW THOUGHT SPIRITUAL TEACHER
AND LIFE COACH

I woke up on the morning of August 5th, our wedding day, and looked out the window. It was a perfect day to get married. Even though it was still early, and the ceremony wasn't until the evening, the sky was already a solid sparkling blue.

"Thank you God!" I said aloud, as I thought about how beautiful the photos would be. Our photographer wanted to take the wedding party pictures outdoors. We had been given the thumbs up by the universe.

My parents and the bridesmaids were meeting at my apartment to get ready. Along with the make-up artist and hairdresser, the photographer, and the flower delivery people, it made for a very tight space in the tiny apartment. As I slipped into my mother's wedding dress in the bedroom, my mother was wrestling with her own dress. I could see her struggling in the hallway.

"I can't get this sleeve to stay up." My mother held out her arm, covered in pink lace, towards my sister, Jennifer. Suddenly my Dad said:

"Jesus Christ Marjie, you can't get anything right. You are incompetent!"

I looked at my mother but she showed no reaction. No facial response; no words to defend herself. Nothing had changed. This was normal for them.

"It's not incompetence, you're just nervous Daddy!" I rebuked him on her behalf. My father scowled as he shook his head.

My mother came into the bedroom and shut the door.

"Julia, I know you said that the reception would be open bar, but your father won't be drinking tonight."

"He won't?" I was surprised. He had helped pay for it with their contribution of more than two thousand dollars.

"No, he won't be." My mother looked me in the eye and shook her head.

"Okay," I murmured. "Will you help me with this hat?"

"Sure, honey." The smile came back to her face and she slid bobby pins into my hair to make sure my hat would remain in place at just the right tilt. I smiled in the mirror and thought 'Wow'. Today would be the day that we would celebrate for the rest of our lives. Someday, our children would celebrate this day with us! We would tell them about it and they would see the pictures. They would see all the bridesmaids, wearing their teal-colored dresses, and their Aunt Jennifer, as the maid of honor, wearing the special flowered pattern dress that their grandmother made. We would tell them, or better yet, they would already know every person in the pictures. They would see their grandparents, their aunts and uncles, and all our special friends.

I looked over at our good friends, the Morettis. Both parents and their two older children, aged five and eight years old, were participating in the wedding.

Tony, Randy's friend for the last 20 years, was the best man. He would be walking down the aisle with my sister, Jennifer. Tony's wife, Anna would be singing the "Wedding Song". Their children would be welcoming guests and handing out programs. I wanted to remember every moment.

The doorbell rang and a second later, Jennifer yelled: "The limo is here!"

This was it! Jennifer held my train up all the way down the stairs.

"I'm going to trip on all this material, Jennifer!"

"I got it, I got it," she yelled back, as if I was stressing about nothing. It seemed like only a few minutes between walking down the stairs and my father walking me down the aisle. All I saw were camera flashes going off. I felt like a movie star and smiled from ear to ear. I looked up to see all the bridesmaids lined up on the left, and the groomsmen lined up on the right. Perfect! Just like we had planned. While walking, I noticed my right leg was shaking. Why was my leg shaking now? Nerves? I was sure no one noticed. We made it to the front of the church without it giving out.

"Who gives this woman to this man?" our petite, blond-haired minister, Eve, asked my father.

"Her mother and I," my father responded, as he placed my hand in Randy's hand. My eyes crinkled as my grin became larger. I looked at Randy and he returned the expression. The tears of joy in his eyes made me tilt my head to one side and nod to let him know I felt the same happiness. I knew I was marrying the best man on earth. Time escaped me and it felt like only seconds before I felt a nudge from the ring bearer. I quickly took Randy's ring and looked up at Eve.

"Repeat after me," she advised, and in segments I completed my vows.

" I, Julia, take you, Randy to be my wedded husband, to have and to hold from this day forward." I struggled to get the ring on his finger. I looked around, smiling at my own dilemma, and made a slightly audible nervous laugh. With Randy's help, the ring finally made it on to his finger. I continued my vows, "for better, for worse, for richer, for poorer, in sickness and in health, to love and to cherish till death do we part."

He succeeded in putting the ring on my finger more smoothly as he said his vows, and then it was done.

Then Eve turned to our guests.

"Friends and family, you occupy an important place in this couple's lives. It is through your company that these two have learned the lessons of friendship, the tremendous act of giving one's love to another, and they ask your blessing as well over their marriage."

I looked at Randy and raised my eyebrows. We hadn't practiced this part. She continued: "Two people in love do not live in isolation. Their love is a source of strength with which they may nourish not only each other but also the world around them. And in turn, you, their community of friends and family, have a responsibility to this couple. Will you, who are present here today, reach out to them in their times of trouble as well as their times of joy and support this marriage always?"

"We will," our guests, answered in unison.

"With these commitments to each other," Eve smiled at both of us, "and from you, friends and family," she looked up at all our guests, "I now pronounce you man and wife, you may kiss your bride!"

The tears in Randy's eyes glistened as we hugged before kissing. Then we locked our lips as the crowd clapped. An overwhelming sense of empathy for Randy filled my being. I was absorbed in the moment and absorbed in his love. We were finally one. Peace and contentment filled my soul.

The reception celebrations were already in full swing when Randy and I arrived. The groomsmen and bridesmaids were being announced as they entered. I found this more exciting than entering the church. I rubbed my hands together as I listened to the crowd clap loudly after each couple entered. When it was time for Randy and me to enter the reception, the Led Zeppelin song "Whole Lotta Love" came on at full volume.

"And finally, I would like to introduce to you, Mr. and Mrs. Randy Castleton!" the D.J. spoke over the music before increasing the volume even more.

Holding hands, we entered the reception dancing and laughing while waving to each table. Someone I didn't know handed me a glass of wine and I gladly accepted it.

I scanned the room looking for my parents. I signaled to Randy that I was going over to their table.

"Mummy!" I exclaimed. She stood up and smiled.

"You're so beautiful honey, I'm so proud of you," she whisper-shouted in my ear. I hugged her, then looking over her shoulder I noticed my father with a full shot glass! Was it whiskey or rum? It didn't appear to be mixed with anything.

"Did you get some appetizers?" I asked, then just to my mother: "I thought you said Daddy wasn't drinking tonight." She backed up and brushed a hair away from my face.

"I don't know. He does what he wants."

"Oh, okay." I squinted at her to show my confusion but didn't say any more. "So, where's Jennifer?"

"She's at the head table. I think they want to get things going." My mother pointed, to the D.J. who was indeed making the announcement for our first dance. I had wanted our first dance to be a country song, but Randy was insistent that we dance to "Wonderful Tonight" by Eric Clapton. I demurred, thinking it was so romantic that he wanted a specific love song. The instrumentals of the song started and our bodies came together and flowed with the music. I put my head on his shoulder as we danced. As I felt his breath on my neck, I knew I was the luckiest person alive. I felt safe, secure and knew that I would be loved eternally by this man, my husband. "How are you doing honey?" he whispered, "Did you see my tears? I think I almost cried earlier."

"Great, I'm doing great," I whispered back. "I can't believe all these people came!" We giggled together and continued to sway back and forth while the flashes went off all around us. We were enjoying every minute of it. Right before the music ended, I melted into his chest and told him how much I loved him.

"And I love you sweetie!" he said, as we held hands and lifted them in the air at the conclusion of the song. We finally made it, I thought. Here we are at our wedding, and all our friends and families are together, having a great time. Life could not get any better.

At that moment, we heard the clanging of silverware on glasses and I whispered in his ear: "I guess they want us to kiss?" I giggled as we kissed at the request of our guests.

"Next we have the father-daughter dance!" The DJ announced as my father smiled and got up to join me. He looked spectacular, in a black tuxedo with a teal-colored bow tie and his black hair combed back. My father didn't like dancing so we had asked the D.J. to fade out the music right after the photographer had taken our picture. So, 'Daddy's Little Girl' started and ended within the same minute.

Randy and his mother danced to a song called 'My Little One.' I looked at them dancing and thought about how lucky we both were to have all our parents still alive for this marvelous occasion. They looked so content, and I wondered if all the things Randy had told me about his bad childhood was hogwash? But then again, one would never guess the challenges I had grown up with either, when my father and I were on show. Maybe we had all grown past the demons of our childhoods, I thought. At least we would be creating glorious futures.

As the flashes of the cameras continued non-stop, I felt like a princess.

The D.J then made an announcement.

"Ladies and Gentlemen. I have a little bit of bad news, at this point. I would like all the women who have keys to Randy's apartment to return them to him at this time." People began to laugh and Randy winked at me and said: "Come on, don't be shy!"

One by one, women of all different ages, mothers, aunts, girlfriends of men that didn't even know Randy, started getting up and delivering keys to him. We laughed whole-heartedly.

"C'mon, any more?" the DJ encouraged.

After about 30 seconds, one of the groomsmen came up and delivered a key to me. I giggled like a teenager.

With my sister, Jennifer, singing her version of Elvis Presley's 'Can't Help Falling in Love,' Tony singing Frank Sinatra's 'Come Fly with Me' and Randy and his buddies singing "Cherie" the laughter, clapping and woo-hoo's didn't stop.

It was just before the last dance that I noticed my parents were missing.

I looked across the room at Jennifer.

"Did Mummy and Daddy leave already?"

"Yes, I think so!" She shook her head.

"Why?"

"Mommy said something about being tired." Jennifer shrugged and continued talking to Brian.

It wouldn't be until years later that I would understand that her "tiredness" was my mother's code for my father's inability to handle alcohol. My mother was an expert at covering for him. I just shook my head and joined my new husband on the dance floor. I wouldn't let them spoil what was a perfect ending to a perfect day, and just the beginning of our perfect life.

CHAPTER 8
RAGE AND IMPULSIVITY

"Impulsive actions led to trouble, and trouble could have unpleasant consequences"

– Stieg Larsson, Swedish journalist and writer.

But it was not to be perfect. The following two years were filled with exciting plans, but also troubling times which sometimes made me wonder if I had married the right man after all.

One evening we were watching a movie on television that depicted a house fire with multiple burn victims. "That poor family!" I exclaimed, as I snuggled next to my new husband. "I would just die if that happened to us. But if it did, I would always stay with you. It wouldn't matter if you had burns over 80% of your body. I would always be here!" I smiled at him and snuggled closer.

"You would?" he looked at me inquisitively. "Hmmm, I wish I could say the same." His gaze went back to the television. I rationalized the statement, telling myself he was just saying that because it was too unfathomable to think about.

His questionable behavior and attitude did not revolve around just our communications: it extended out to the world at large. I recognized he did not like people in general. There was the time, we were coming home from the movies and saw a couple of people stranded on the side of the road. The reason was obvious. Their car had a flat tire. The driver and passenger were both inspecting the wheel.

"Pull over, Randy! They need help. Let's give them our can of Fix-a-Flat. It will at least get them to the nearest gas station!"

"Jesus, Julia, I'm not here to save the world!" he countered as if I had asked him to give up a kidney.

"Randy, look at them, if you were in that position, wouldn't you want someone to help you?"

"Well, I'm not and you shouldn't be forcing your choices on me." He did pull over.

I happily provided the emergency can to the couple but Randy and I didn't speak for the following two days. He didn't want me changing his attitude and I didn't want him changing mine.

Within a few months after we were married, he came home steaming about the directors of his workplace.

"Those assholes, they don't know what they're doing. I know way more than they do! Pulling me into their office and acting like I caused personnel problems. Well, they can go to hell!"

I never did find out the cause of the quarrel. Randy didn't say but he and his employer came to a "mutual agreement" that he would leave within a month.

Randy seemed to have more of these types of issues than most people. It was as if he felt the world was out to get him. He was angry with the world for that and angry with me because I didn't see things the same way.

Those issues aside, we had good times as well. We had already started creating our own annual traditions, and one of them was running the New York Boilermaker 15 kilometer road race. That year, I decided to run it last minute, ignoring the fact that I was completely unprepared. We stood at the starting line together as he looked at me and smiled.

"Oh you poor, impetuous, brave, little munchkin...you poor, foolish, misguided, courageous little munchkin!" Every time he repeated it and added a new adjective, we would both crack up laughing so hard we could barely stand up. Our laughter reminded me of all our good times and made me forget everything else.

After a couple of brutally cold New England winters, we had decided to move to sunny Florida where Randy wanted to earn a doctorate degree while I supported us financially.

Our second wedding anniversary had passed without any drama. The heat was extreme that summer, topping out at 97 degrees, and I was thankful to have air conditioning in our apartment unit. It wasn't common for homes in New Hampshire to have air conditioning. Our neighbors were going to the movies for the air conditioning alone to escape the heatwave. The humidity was stifling and it was sapping just to walk out to the parking lot to get into my boiling hot car.

Of course, the temperatures in Florida would be even higher, and I wasn't looking forward to being indoors most of the time. I would be leaving my family and friends, but I knew this was what I needed to do as a proper loving wife. I was excited too. I would have warmth in the winter months, new places to discover, new friends, and a new job.

It had been a busy summer so far. I had quit my job in May to finish my master's degree program. In July, Randy had traveled for two weeks for Military Reserve training, and I had been gone another week to volunteer as a camp counselor for my church. Randy had been very upset by my decision to volunteer and gave me the cold shoulder when I came back. I chose not to react. Volunteering was part of who I was and I planned to continue it. Life did not slow down in August and we still needed to pack for the movers.

With the small wall-mounted air conditioner blowing on our backs, we began stowing away items from our wedding in the boxes that we had purchased for the move. I was making small talk as I pulled out a scrapbook for our first five years of marriage "We need to add some pictures to this, Randy.....maybe of the big move, to cover the year of our second anniversary! "

Randy shook his head and said: "You know what I have a real problem with?"

I looked up. "What?"

His tone had sounded angry. Now I realized it matched his expression.

"You. Just taking off for a week, just for fun!" So he wasn't letting that go.

"I wanted to do it." I shrugged.

"Yeah, well, I know you told your mother: 'I can volunteer for a week, because Randy took off for two weeks last month'."

I looked down at the glassware I had begun wrapping and thought to myself 'why did he talk to my mother about this', and then I wondered why I had even talked to my mother? She did seem to side frequently with Randy on these types of disagreements. Sometimes I felt Randy really needed a "traditional" wife – a wife that would stay home and cook and clean for him - and my mother was the archetypal "traditional" wife, so perhaps she understood him more than she understood me.

I remembered calling to tell her I had finally passed my CPA exam the previous summer, after three attempts.

"Mummy, I have great news! Guess what it is! Guess, guess!" I had said.

"Are you pregnant honey?" was her response.

"Pregnant? No, no, much better than that." I muttered into the phone, my excitement drying up.

"I can't imagine what then, honey. What?"

"I finally passed the CPA exam!" I tried to fill my voice with the original excitement I had felt, expecting her to ask me all about it, and what it meant now. But she didn't.

"Oh, that's nice, honey," was all she said. I could tell by her tone that she was disappointed I wasn't pregnant.

"Tell Daddy!" I had shouted into the phone. I knew my father would be more excited for me, because he seemed to have more of an understanding of academia and careers. She said she would, but then hung up.

I stared at the wrapped glassware with Randy standing over me.

"I don't know why you talked to my mother about me volunteering at a summer camp, but if I want to go to a camp for a week, I can. It's my life."

Randy started physically shaking and I saw the perspiration beads on his forehead. I knew he was furious. He threw down the frying pan that he had been packing and left the room in an obvious rage, but then returned within minutes.

"Ya know, I really don't like being married.......if I had the chance to do it all over again, I wouldn't marry you."

I looked at him dismayed. "What a terrible thing to say!"

His shaking stopped, the perspiration was no longer visible, and he was suddenly as calm as a Buddhist monk. "I'm not saying that to hurt you; I mean it."

His sudden change in demeanor, like many times before, was still startling to me. It was as if his verbal jab, that hit me below the belt, gave him a sudden sense of relief. I wondered what I had gotten myself into by committing to move to Florida with him. I no longer had a place to live in New Hampshire, or a job, or any money, and now the man I had quit everything for was telling me he didn't like being married to me. He didn't want to be married to me.

I did the only thing I could think of doing. I got up, packed a small bag of clothes and my sleeping bag, and left the apartment. I slept on a friend's floor that night as I contemplated my options. He didn't need to tell me twice.

The next day I returned to the apartment when I knew Randy would be out, to collect some more things.

I found a note from him, apologizing for saying he wouldn't marry me again. Randy said he knew it was "wrong and irresponsible". I found it telling that he did not say he was sorry for deeply hurting me. My emotional well-being rarely seemed to enter his mind. He just lashed out like an angry child whenever he wanted to.

Later that evening, Randy and I sat on the beige-carpeted floor in the living room because the furniture had plastic wrap around it all already. I was quiet and waited for him to speak, feeling that I deserved a much bigger apology. Finally, he stood up and crossed his arms.

"Things built up. I got really frustrated with you and I just blew up. I'm sorry."

He didn't look sorry. His face had no expression and he seemed detached.

"I don't get it Randy. You don't stab someone in the heart like that and then just say 'Sorry, I blew up' like it was no big deal. I need to know where that came from."

He looked at me with narrowed eyes as if I should already know. "You're not my ideal woman," he confirmed.

As I looked at him with astonishment, he proceeded to list the traits that his ideal woman would have.

"I want a woman who is thin, good-looking, well-educated, professional, not shy in bed, athletic, enjoys cleaning house and is good at decorating the house. You certainly don't meet the last two. You don't like cleaning or decorating. You are just not ideal."

Was he kidding me? I stared at him. "Are you serious?"

"Of course I'm serious!"

"I'm not sure what I am more surprised by: the fact that you actually have a list of female traits that make up your ideal woman, two years after you and I got married, or the fact that you think I should like cleaning house and decorating. Why? Because I'm female?"

"All my friends have wives that like to clean and decorate. Why don't you?"

"All of your friends do? Randy, you are acting like a child! You think cleaning and decorating are my responsibilities because I'm female? No. That is not the case." I rolled my eyes at him in disgust.

Randy actually bared his teeth, and I saw his facial muscles tense up. "I want you to know I used to have it much better than this! My ex-girlfriend, Lindsey, used to cook, clean and decorate our house!"

"Then why didn't you stay with her? Maybe you should have!" I yelled at him now.

"She didn't have all the qualities I wanted. But, there are lots of women out there that have all those qualities, that I could have any time if I wanted to!"

"Maybe it is time you realized you're not perfect yourself!" I countered.

I stood up, grabbed my journal and left the apartment, slamming the door on my way out. I realized my journal was more of a trusted companion than my husband.

The fact that this, and many similar fights throughout our marriage, were indicative of emotional abuse didn't occur to me. It wouldn't be until many years later that I would come to understand that, and that I had been groomed, throughout my entire childhood, to tolerate and love my abuser regardless.

This time though, I didn't forgive and forget. It was as if a part of me had finally had enough. He was too cold, too mean, and showed no remorse or empathy. Women were just pawns in his chess game, and he was playing to win. I started to realize that this personality flaw in Randy, which showed itself as selfishness and narcissism, was not reparable, even by me.

But I was in a conundrum. I had no place to live, no job, no income of any sort, and a man who made it clear that he no longer loved me. And we were supposed to be moving in two days. All I could think to do was to write. I parked my blue 89 Toyota Tercel under a large oak tree and, sitting in the driver's seat, I began to write in my journal.

I wrote about life, love, loss and missed opportunities. I wrote about the fights with Randy, his words that cut like knives, and, as I reflected upon missed opportunities, I thought of another guy, Kevin.

I had met Kevin at the summer camp where we were both volunteers. We had shared several late night talks together and had developed a friendship. He seemed so sweet, authentic and real; so unlike the present-day Randy. What might have happened if I were not married? Nothing had happened, as I took my marriage vows very seriously, but I couldn't help but wonder, what if I wasn't married? What if I had been single?

But I realized I was already committed; committed to Randy and committed to moving to Florida. However I felt, he was my husband.

Like my mother, I would stick with the man I had married, regardless of his behavior and the words that came out of his mouth. I stashed the memory of our fights to the back of my mind, and decided I would return to the apartment with a positive attitude, and just hope for the best. I drove back to our home where very few items remained: my fireproof safe, which I used to lock up irreplaceable items such as old photographs, my passport, and my savings account passbook; a gym bag full of clothes that should last the week it took to drive south, and a little bit of food on the kitchen counter. I stashed the journal in the safe as it seemed to be the most appropriate and secure place for it.

A day later, Randy broke into the safe.

I was studying at the library when he called the librarian and told her there was an emergency at home. My mind went into a panic. Clearly he was alive as he had made the call. Were my parents still alive? My siblings? His parents? Had there been a car accident? What horrible timing, the day before our move! I drove home, barely able to concentrate on the road. The tires squealed as I turned into the parking lot and ran up the stairs to our apartment. Out of breath, I looked at Randy, in the hope of being able to read his face, to find out who had died or who was at a hospital.

"What happened, what happened?" The worry on my face must have been evident from my wide eyes.

"I read your journal and I am leaving for Florida without you! You fucking stay here with Kevin! I don't care what the hell you do!"

Randy's furious eyes met mine and I saw again what I can only describe as evil - and desperation.

"No! I love you!" I tried to reassure him. "I love our marriage; I want all of our plans to work out, and I want to be with you!"

"Well Julia, you screwed up!" He shouted, and then, as if feeling more empowered, he added: "You had a good thing and now you lost it!"

He ripped his wedding ring from his hand, crushed the ring with a hammer that we had been using to take nails out of the wall, and threw it at me across the empty living room. "See what you've caused! See? You did this!" The anger seemed to be pouring out of every cell in his body.

I was flabbergasted. I knew I hadn't written anything that would warrant throwing away a marriage, and that was the very reason I hadn't done anything. I didn't want to destroy our marriage. Although I understood the reason he was hurt, I didn't understand why he was acting as if I had actually cheated on him.

"I did what, Randy? I didn't do anything!" I retorted, as I backed away from where the crushed ring had landed.

"Then prove it. Cut off your friendship with Kevin completely, now, and maybe I will change my mind!" He grabbed the phone from the wall and handed it to me. "You call him, in front of me, and you tell him that you are cutting off his friendship!"

"No!" I yelled, as I stepped closer to him and pointed at him to make that clear.

"You will!" The veins pulsating in his neck showed me his level of fury.

"No! I will not! You are crazy!" I screamed.

"You call him now, or else…or else…you are not going to Florida with me!"

"Then I am not going with you!" I shouted. "You are not going to control me like that! You will never control me!"

Every time I spoke, he became angrier. It reminded me of my father, storming through my childhood home while my mother cried in the bathroom. I had decided at that point, 18 years earlier, that I would never cower to rage-filled men. I couldn't help but wonder to myself, out of all the men in the world, how had I ended up with one that had the same anger issues that my father had? The same desire to control me; the same nasty words and the same disgusting attitude. The only difference was my father needed alcohol to induce the ugly person hidden inside him, while Randy just needed to feel the fear of being alone.

I still didn't want to give up on everything though. How could we possibly give up the marriage, the move, the money already invested in the move, and his opportunity to go to school at Florida State University? I wanted us both to calm down. As we stood in the empty living room, with the crushed wedding ring on the clean carpet between us, I lowered my voice.

"Randy, I love you, but I'm not going to be controlled by you. I want to go to Florida and I want us to continue with the plans we made." I looked at him and waited. Taking my lead, he refrained from the loud volume.

"It's not going to work out. It's just not going to." He shook his head.

"Well, I'm going to my last class tomorrow, as I planned, and I hope you wait for me and we can head down south afterwards together." I anticipated there was still a part of him that wanted to stick with our original plan, to take our individual cars and follow each other on the road.

"No, I'm leaving while you are in class." His voice was cold and indifferent.

"Okay. Well I hope you change your mind." My sadness was obvious and my hope was real.

That night, we both slept in our separate sleeping bags on the living room floor and I got up early and headed to class.

When class finished, I walked out of the building, half expecting him to be there and half knowing he wouldn't be. Walking down the large granite steps, my anxiety increased as I accepted the fact that whatever I did see in the next few minutes would determine the rest of my life. At the last step that opened up to the sidewalk, I looked up and around.

There was no car waiting for me by the curbside; no Randy.

Sadness and anger filled my body equally. Part of me was very sad that Randy thought so little of our marriage that he would let something so small and inconsequential wreck our plans. The other part of me wasn't surprised that Randy would go to this extreme, to purposely upset me, and this incensed me.

However, as I walked to the parking lot, I did recognize the man standing by my car.

Tony Moretti. Randy's best man. I was puzzled. As I got closer he said: "He's gone, Julia. He left for Florida without you."

Then he took me into his arms as tears rolled down my cheeks.

"I know," I whimpered. "I just don't understand him."

I was so grateful Tony was there. I had no idea why he was, but he suggested we take a walk around the campus and then he explained how Randy had told him that I was cheating and keeping secrets and he was leaving.

"But I didn't........."

"I know Julia, he has a problem." We both knew he had a problem.

Tony knew I had no place to go.

"Come over to our house tonight and stay for a few days. Take some time to figure things out. Randy is being an ass; he's been lying and deceitful with me, and he's manipulative. You don't deserve him."

I stayed at the Moretti's house that night and Tony, his wife Anna and I, sat at their kitchen table and talked for hours. Both listened like the good therapists I didn't have. I told them about the fights, the crushed wedding ring and his ultimatum to me.

"You're not crazy, Julia. He's crazy." Anna counseled me.

Tony asked: "Has he hit you?"

"What?" I couldn't believe he was asking me that.

"Has he physically harmed you?" Anna reworded her husband's question to me.

"No, he hasn't hit me! Don't you think I would have told you that by now?"

Why were they asking? Did they know something that I didn't know? Did he have a past that included hitting women; a past that included hitting anybody? Tony had known Randy since they were in high school together.

"Why do you ask?"

"We just wanted to make sure you were safe." Tony shook his head as if he meant nothing by the question. But it didn't feel like it was a question borne of nothing. It felt like there was a reason.

Anna told me that while Randy was visiting his friend in Maine that summer, they had both gone out to a bar to see if they could pick up women.

"Are you sure?" I asked.

I couldn't believe what I was hearing. I had spent that weekend at home, taking care of our dogs. I was always supportive of Randy maintaining his friendships. It was around the time of our second wedding anniversary and we weren't fighting at all; not even a small argument.

"Julia, I am sure. He told Tony himself! And Randy told him he had gone out to one woman's truck and fooled around with her."

"Oh my God. On top of all this, he cheated on me?" My mouth dropped open.

"Oh, there's more, Julia. There's more you don't know about." Anna confessed how terrible she felt, divulging this information, but she said she didn't want to see me manipulated and lied to by Randy. I begged her to tell me everything she knew, but she wouldn't tell me anymore. "I'm sorry, Julia. I promised not to say anything......but I wanted you to know what you're dealing with, so I told you that part."

I called my parents to let them know I was safe and with the Moretti's. That call set the scene for what happened next. Later that night Randy also called my parents and my mother told him where I was. He reversed direction in New Jersey, after driving six hours south, and drove six hours back, to pull into the Moretti's driveway in the middle of night.

Tony and Anna did not allow him into the house. Randy pounded on the windows and doors, demanding to be let in, telling them that I was his wife and that their friendship was over. Thankfully their three young children slept through all of it. Tony told him to leave or else they would call the police. He left, but not before hollering through the door that he was leaving our dogs in my car which was parked in the driveway. Although I was thrilled to see both dogs, I knew I had no place to live for me or for them. Randy was just trying to make life as difficult as possible. It was a punishment.

I wasn't convinced then (or now) that I knew all of Randy's past. But I do know that on that night, both my two year marriage to Randy, and their twenty year friendship with him, were over for good.

I would reconsider out of guilt and sadness. But in my heart, as of that night, I never wanted him back. 'Who was this person I had married?' 'Who was this person that I had quit my entire life in New Hampshire for?' He was a liar, a cheater, an abuser, and potentially violent on top of it all. Even the cold, hardwood chair that I was sitting on in Tony and Anna's kitchen couldn't compare to the coldness we would all experience from Randy in the following months.

He added to my debt, cut off my health insurance and threatened my friends and me. I lived every day in a state of shock. I had nothing except a small bag of clothing and a six year-old car, that I hoped would last another few years. The one thing I was very grateful for was my career.

I remembered something my father had told me many years before. It was while I was struggling with some trigonometry problems as a senior in high school, and wondering out loud if I could survive calculus in college. "You know Daddy," I said, "not everyone goes to college."

"Honey," my father looked at me, very seriously, and his voice was slow, as if he wanted me to take my time and let every word sink in. "You could lose everything you have; your house, your car, your possessions, anything and everything ....but if you get an education, no one can take that away from you. It's the one thing that you will always have, regardless of what happens to you."

How prophetic. He was right. I knew I would be okay because I had an education. He and my mother had made sure of that. Despite all the problems of my childhood, I had to be grateful to my parents for making a college education a priority for all of us.

Over the coming months, the need to make good decisions became imperative. I would find out those decisions would even mean the difference between life and death.

For now I didn't know where Randy had gone but I didn't care. I called my parents to let them know what had happened.

"Mummy is that you?"

"Yes, honey. It's me." Her voice seemed to crack.

"I just wanted to let you know Randy has gone over the deep end. He was here at 3 AM last night demanding to see me, and he put the dogs in my car even though I have no place to go with them! But don't worry, I am safe and the dogs are too."

My mother interrupted me. "Honey, he's here. He's sleeping upstairs right now. He - is – just - a -wreck!" She choked out the last five words before taking a deep, audible, inhalation of breath.

"He's what? You aren't serious!" I took a gulp of coffee that Anna had put down in front of me as I paced the kitchen. "You gave him a place to sleep! What are you thinking?" I felt immediate betrayal. I felt no compassion for the no man's land that my mother suddenly found herself in. "I am your daughter, and you not only tell him where I am without asking me, but you take him in!"

I heard my mother sniffle.

"It was…it was…3:30 this morning, and he had no place to go……"

"I have no place to go! Because of him!"

I was furious, but I was whispering into the phone while pacing the kitchen, as all three Moretti children were still sleeping in nearby rooms.

It had been a trauma-filled night. I had called Kevin earlier to advise him that Randy was behaving unpredictably due to reading my journal and learning of our friendship.

"Oh, I know," Kevin confirmed to me. "He called me in the middle of the night, threatening me, telling me that he wanted to know exactly what was going on between you and me. I told him the truth: I said 'nothing', and that you and I were just fond of each other. Then he said he had half a mind to come up here and beat the shit out of me……yep, he said he wanted to resolve it, man-to-man, by beating the shit out of me."

"I am so sorry, so sorry…….." was all I could mutter to Kevin. Now, as I talked to my mother, I added up the number of people whose lives were being turned upside down by Randy.

"Mummy, please stop. Do not support him." I begged her. I assumed he had told my parents the essence of what I had written in my journal, so it didn't completely surprise me that she saw him as the victim.

"He's just hurt, honey. He needs your help. You two have planned this move for so long. Don't ruin it now." Her voice cracked again.

I stared at the floor in a daze. I rubbed my shoulders and became defensive.

"Mummy, I am not ruining anything! He is not stable, and if you were here last night, you would agree. He is dangerous. Just know that I am safe. I will be with the Morettis all day in Boston to hide from him. Please do not tell Randy where we are. But while we are gone, he does need to come back and get the dogs. They will be waiting safely in the air-conditioned enclosed porch with water. He needs to come get them. Please don't tell him where we are. The Moretti's don't feel safe either. They almost had to call the cops last night!"

"He is devastated by both you and the Morettis turning your backs on him when he needs you. Come home and talk to him. You can bring the dogs here. Stop listening to the Morettis. I know they think they are helping, but they aren't!"

"I am not coming anywhere near you until he's gone," I cried, while trying not to shout too loud. After a tearful conversation, my mother agreed that he would be gone if I came home.

"Well, I have to go" I muttered. "I'll call you tonight to let you know what I am doing."

I called my mother later from a payphone in Boston and found out that Randy did pick up the dogs and took them to my parent's house. He would be spending the next night with some friends who lived about an hour away.

During that night, his friends convinced him that his life was now down in Florida. Indeed it was: his apartment, our furniture, all of his clothing, everything he owned and his schooling which was starting that week. I was relieved to hear that he had left the state, and after a couple of days, I headed back to my hometown to stay with my parents.

I contemplated keeping our dogs, but felt that if we ended up in court arguing about them, they would be seen as property and he might receive one dog and I would receive one dog. I didn't have the heart to break them up. They had known only each other their whole lives, and I knew Randy and I both treated them very well. On top of this, I didn't have the resources needed to look after them now, with no job, no money and no apartment. The sluggish economy in my area made me uncertain how long it would take to land a job, especially as an entry level accountant.

Three days after he left, Randy called my mother and asked her to fly the dogs down. I felt like he was treating my mother as his own mother, as someone that he could talk to for support and vent his frustrations to. Plus she sided with him, and even asked me to help her with the formalities for my dogs.

Looking back, it was so easy to see the markers that our marriage was doomed from the start. But while I was in it, facing those hurdles, it just seemed like normal relationship difficulties. It was obvious Randy felt no remorse and had no empathy for others.

There had been so many unprovoked jealous reactions that I had stashed to the back of my mind. On our honeymoon, he didn't speak to me for two days because I was nice to the waiter on the cruise ship. On that same trip, he became enraged with me for telling a couple that we met, who were also on their honeymoon, that I looked forward to watching the husband in a talent show that evening. He was jealous of someone else's husband!

He thought nothing of going through my personal belongings, as if I wasn't entitled to any privacy.

The out of control violence wasn't just limited to jealousy. Once, he got so angry he flipped over the dining room table and cleared our counter tops with one full swoop of his arm. It was less than a week after we married, and my parents were coming over to go out to dinner with us. I had been looking for a job with an accounting firm and Randy had known someone that seemed like a good contact. When the attempted connection didn't work out, I was frustrated.

"Okay, no more help. I'm going to a headhunter next."

"What the hell! Then find your own job. I was only trying to help you!" Then he exploded, like a grenade in a war zone. Things flew by my face, missing me by inches; pens, pencils, and text books from the table, and the cutting board that had been left out on the kitchen counter from an earlier meal. I ran into the living room to escape the missiles.

"Stop it! Stop it!" I screamed, sounding just like my mother from years before. "My parents are coming over! Look what they are going to see!"

Randy then stormed out of the apartment. As I heard his car screeching out of the parking lot, I dialed my parents to tell them not to bother coming. There was no answer, which meant it was too late to stop them. When they arrived and saw the results of Randy's temper tantrum, my parents just started picking everything up off the floor.

"It's okay honey, it's okay. Let's get this stuff put away."

My father tried to calm me down.

"No, don't do that!" I grabbed a decorative candle from my father's hand and threw it back on the floor: "Randy did this and Randy is going to clean it up!" Later that evening, Randy did clean up the mess, after realizing I wasn't going to take care of it. He gave me the cold shoulder for two days.

My mind was mired in memories, but I was back in my parents' house and it was time to carve out a new future. Meanwhile my mother was trying to call Randy to talk about the dog's flights. She got a busy signal all day.

That night I said to her: "Mummy, you know why it's busy constantly, right?"

"No!" She looked at me, momentarily closing her eyes as if to say: 'What now?'

"He is on his way back to New Hampshire to get me." She closed her eyes shaking her head, "Julia, you are so paranoid."

"I just know him," I answered. "But it will be a wasted journey. He went too far."

My father, not wanting to see my hurt, interrupted us. "It's going to be a nice day tomorrow, why don't we all take a trip to the mountains?"

I thanked him but said no. I knew what the morning would bring.

At 8:30 AM the house phone rang, and I heard my mother pick it up. I cracked my bedroom door open to hear more clearly.

"Hello? I didn't believe Julia, but she knows you so well!"

I took a deep breath and went down the stairs, but my father got to my mother first, took the phone from her and to my surprise said: "Randy, you and your phone calls are not welcome here anymore." Then he hung up.

I was stunned. It seemed my father, at least, had recognized that the man I had married was unpredictable and irrational, and as my mother always took my father's lead, I felt she too would come to understand, and support me.

Two days later, Randy called my parents' house again. My sister, Jennifer, was visiting and picked up the phone. Jennifer told me later that he was as calm as a cucumber and wanted to let me know he was interested in reconciling.

"What? That's what he said to you? Does he want me to say: "Oh sure Randy, why not? I'll get back with you! No problem!"

"He tries to be charming, but I don't fall for it. I know Mommy falls for it and he's good at it; he acts so sweetly, like he's the reasonable one and you're the crazy one!"

That had always been his game. It used to confuse me; how he could go from being in a complete state of rage to cool, calm and collected within a very short period of time. But that was the Jekyll and Hyde in him.

CHAPTER 9
WELL-INTENDED BAD ADVICE

"Well-intended bad advice is like a monkey seeing a fish in a lake, and thinking the fish is drowning, rushes over to pull it out of the water so it can place it safely in a tree."

– Unknown

Living at home, at the age of 28, was sobering and not what I had planned. However, the time away from Randy allowed me to see things much more clearly than I had in the past. I knew I should have left a long time before, and not even married a person like him. I blamed myself, and cringed inside, that I had accepted his abusive traits as normal. But all I had wanted was someone who loved me, and a happy marriage. Now I tried to be positive about the change of direction in my life, but sadness and depression would descend like a dark cloud.

I still wanted the house, the white picket fence, dogs, and maybe even kids. I had dreamed of us going to church as a family on Sundays and opening presents at Christmas. I dreamed of family vacations and Thanksgiving dinners. As every day passed that August, I seemed to be moving further and further from my dreams.

I would just sit, write in my journal and cry, until I had no tears left. My dogs would lay next to me and comfort me.

My mother peeked her head into my bedroom as I wiped the tears from my face with my hands.

"I really think you should call Randy. I hate to see you in so much pain; both of you. He called me and told me that he's willing to go to counseling with you."

I closed my eyes and took a deep breath. As I exhaled, I opened them to see my mother sitting on the end of my bed. Her curved back and rounded shoulders gave me the impression that she felt like the victim in the whole ordeal, rather than me. I didn't have any strength left to treat her with kid gloves.

"Counseling with me? No, Mother, this has gone way beyond the point of counseling. He is crazy, he is dangerous, and yes, I am very, very sad that this is happening, but counseling with me is not going to help him."

I went on as her shoulders sagged still further: "Mother, he has threatened other people. He has abandoned me and is completely disrespectful to me and his own friends. Now, he's trying to pull you over to his side – somehow convincing you that this is my fault."

My mother's eyes, which seemed to be in a permanent state of red lately, filled with tears. "It's not too late. You can still go to Florida with him and the dogs. He wants to go to Florida, so you can still make this work."

I raised my voice: "I cannot make this work; I cannot help him. Me going to Florida would just separate me from everyone that I know. I had almost no support in New Hampshire. How much support do you think I would have in Florida? I have no friends in Florida, Mummy. No friends. I would be miserable. He is sick, mother, don't you see, sick!"

Her voice started to quiver. "He is your husband; you should want to help him. You married him, and promised to love him through sickness and in health!" She emphasized the word 'sickness'.

"No, no, don't give me that. I want to help me, Mother! I need to protect me. Why don't you understand that?" My own tears fell now. "I've wasted enough time, just about my entire twenties, on Randy, and for what? This? For someone that I am embarrassed to say treats me and others horrendously, switches between moods like a light switch, is completely unpredictable…and…and…I don't want to go to Florida and waste even more years that I can't get back. I'll be trapped."

I expected more attempts to force me to take Randy back, but instead my mother brought her hand up to rub her neck as she said: "You do have our support honey. Both your father and I just want you to be happy."

I did not have time to thank her before she added: "That's why we want you to stick with your Florida plans."

"No!" I shook my head. It didn't matter that my mother was refusing to see my side. I had Jennifer's support, and even Kevin's, who amazingly was still willing to speak to me after Randy's threats.

I stood up and started looking around the room for my car keys, knowing I needed to get away from this claustrophobic atmosphere.

"I'm going to visit Susan," I said.

Susan and I had been best friends in high school, but had gone separate ways after attempting to be college roommates during our freshman year. We had handled the adjustment from high school to college very differently. To "fail out" had never been an option for me. I carried the expectations of my parents on my shoulders. Any grades were fine – but failing due to lack of effort was not an option. I studied while Susan partied, and as a result I returned for sophomore year while Susan transitioned to real life. She, like me, had made poor selections in men in her life, and had ended up single with three children, living in a mobile home park. Later that day, I pulled into her dirt driveway and she came out smiling. Her long dark hair reminded me of the two of us in high school, using our curling irons to get ready for double dates. It was hard not to notice the additional body fat trying to squeeze itself out of her clothing. What appeared to be sunburn may have been rosacea.

"It's so good to see you!" She hugged me tightly. It felt so nice to be welcomed with unconditional love. Despite my parents' having some good qualities, I never felt totally welcome in their home.

"Come in, come in. Would you like a soda?"

Her children were running around inside the large caravan, teasing each other and pulling faces.

"Sure, a Coke would be great!" I sat down on the corner couch that took up most of the living room and wondered how one adult and three children could possibly exist in such a tiny space, as Susan poured the coke into a glass.

"So, tell me what's going on." She pointed to the freezer. "Ice?" I nodded yes.

"Oh Susan," I began. "It's a disaster". I told her everything that had happened to date.

"God, Julia, I am so sorry. He seemed like such a nice guy. Are you depressed? You didn't even have kids?"

"Depressed? At not having kids? No! I am thankful, so thankful. Why would I want to add children to this chaotic situation, with a father like him?"

"Well, we are in our late twenties. We aren't getting any younger," Susan chided.

"So, I should have harnessed his sperm while I had the chance? No thanks," was all I could muster, but I quickly lowered my voice as her five year-old boy ran behind my chair. I was too late.

"Sperm! Sperm!" he yelled at the top of his young lungs, laughing. I gave Susan an inquisitive look as if to ask 'does he know what sperm is?'

"He comes out with the strangest things" she laughed.

"I'm not strange!" the little boy hollered as he ran from one side of the mobile home to the other.

I couldn't believe Susan could see my being childless as a loss, when I saw it as one of the biggest blessings. Months later, I would be reminded of the conversation with Susan, as my mother shared her belief that a baby would have held us together. She felt it was part of the reason the marriage had failed.

I knew I needed to make better decisions than the ones that had put Susan in a mobile home park.

I arrived home to find a white envelope on my pillow. In my mother's handwriting were the words: "To my Julia". I recoiled, expecting more of the same advice, but I laid down on the bed and opened the envelope carefully. I began to read my mother's broken script:

Dear Julia,
I'm making my last "wish" on paper, cause you know me, I'm a cry baby and get so emotional, and never can come across the way I want to.

I started to "think" about my notes on my walk this morning – Well now I sit here and pour out my heart to you. I'm not trying to depress you – Lord knows you're already depressed.

There are a few thoughts that have come popping in and out of my mind – which weighs more – the length of good times or the bad times------

Is the marriage worth it to give a second chance – it doesn't cost anything except a bit of time. Now that the demon has been shown (what the real problem is) then maybe it will be easier to deal with.

After all the feedback from the Morettis and from yours truly, for what it's worth – and you know what Jennifer's has said – Divorce him – but some feelings she does not understand.
Back to feedback – there's one more important one – your Heart – only you know what vibes it's sending.

Since he's willing for therapy – then the therapist will see his problem and will also see where you're coming from,. It would be he/her that will tell you what is really the right direction for that. All of the plans and dreams, and your marriage and family (pups), shouldn't have a price tag on it – they are priceless. Aren't they worth fighting for? You can't lose anything for trying --- look what there is to gain.

Knowing how far to rock bottom Randy went, this would be a sure test if ever there was one for him to try, and then if that doesn't work – you will know you have done everything possible.

As far as having someone to talk to when you're new there – Julia, that has never been a problem with you (smiles) which I am grateful for – once you find a job – there will be plenty of friends – And you wouldn't need them right away cause you'll be too busy working on the problem anyway.

I can understand Randy's calling for someone to talk to, cause there is no one for him except himself and yours truly, and I do a lousy job of it. And that is so sad. So what if he needs you in his weird way, like having to be with a female – you are his "female" and wife. We all need each other in some crazy ways – that's what makes the world go round – would be funny if everyone was alike wouldn't it?

You said it might be a waste of a lot of your life (something like that) to try but that would only be a little drop compared to your whole life time. Life is so short and we need all the greatness we can get.

You know in every marriage it seems there is one partner who "needs" the other more and there is nothing wrong with that – feel happy that you are the one he needs and you and Randy are the ones the pups love ---

A "Wish"

If you did try, and it failed, you will never feel any doubt if you did the right thing or not, and that you gave it your "all". Instead though, if you went ahead with the divorce, you may feel a guilt later on in life if you were to marry again (wondering if you did give it your all --------) There would always be that doubt hanging over your head --- That would not be fair to yourself in the future.

You have proved your point by holding back, and in his way Randy has hit rock bottom and suffered, as you in other ways suffered just as much. His actions were horrible but it wasn't the Randy you know and married.

It would be hard work for both partners but the reward would be great!

I would appreciate it if you didn't share this with Jennifer, cause she would only say I was trying to persuade you against what she would like to see happen – Well, maybe I am (pleading a "wish"). All this is because I love you my daughter and you are a very good friend that I can share my feelings with –

Go to that quiet place and pour your thoughts out to yourself and please contact Randy – I won't mention any more again,

Love you,
Mom

Tears welled up in my eyes. I couldn't protect myself and make my mother happy at the same time. I never could. My mind wandered back to all the times I had disappointed her by trying to fix things. There were the times I had hollered at Daddy and made her run into the bathroom and cry; all the fights and the screaming and the hitting, and the times I didn't keep the family fights a secret, like I was supposed to. I remembered how happy my mother was on my wedding day; probably the happiest I had ever seen her. It was the only day in my life that my mother had told me she was proud of me. Now, I was ruining that as well.

It would be another 20 years before I would learn about the development of the role of the "caregiver" within dysfunctional families. I read a fantastic book called "Out of The Fog" by Dana Morningstar. She explained that in any family the rescuer is always someone who is empathetic, self-sacrificing, deferential, willing to put other's needs before their own, uncomfortable with conflict, generous, and perfectionistic.

It was only then that I would realize that my mother's biggest disappointment was that I wasn't going to be the caregiver to Randy that she had been to my father.

CHAPTER 10
GOOD ADVICE

"Good advice usually works best when preceded by a bad scare."

— **Al Batt,** WRITER, SPEAKER, STORYTELLER AND HUMORIST.

As the weeks that I spent away from Randy turned into months, I struggled to bring normalcy back to my life. The problem was I didn't feel I had a life anymore. It was as if Randy had taken my entire identity. Before, I had seen myself as a loving wife, an entry level accountant, a member of an exclusive health club, a member of a church that I enjoyed, and a friend to many. These identities had disappeared in the time that we had been apart and getting them back was my top priority.

Sometimes, when I was really low, I would talk to Kevin. I saw Kevin as the definition of normal. He was cool and calm and spoke of normal things, like work, his house, his plans for future hikes in the woods, and his parents, who lived within driving distance. I envied his stability and the routine of his life.

While at my parent's house, I was living in a house of mirrors. What I felt was unsafe, I was being told was safe. What I felt was hateful, I was being told was loving, and what I felt was incomprehensible, I was being told was understandable, given the circumstances.

My mother continued to have Randy's back, and although my father didn't state his position verbally again, my mother would state all of her desires using the word 'we', implying that both she and my father were in agreement.

My father would get his bad moods like before. One moment he would be calm and concerned for my well-being, then he would blow up at me for not helping my mother with household tasks. It was the childhood script all over again.

I felt like I was in the witness protection program, having been completely removed from one life and dropped into a new one, in a new community. I was trying so hard to fill in all the blanks.

Kevin said I should get out more.

"Julia, go for a walk in the woods, go for a swim in the lake. Do anything to lift your spirits. I think you're getting more and more depressed, and you need to do something about it!"

I lay on my bed like a fifteen year-old, playing with the phone cord as if I was all the way back then, talking to boys I shouldn't be speaking with. I imagined Kevin's crew cut hair and the way his blue eyes had looked at me when we had shared our conversations earlier that summer. I felt a yearning for his company.

"I know, I know. I feel depressed and I'm sorry that it's impacting on you. I'm so sorry for pulling you down."

"It's just that I don't like seeing you like this. You used to be so happy and now you're so sad all the time. Come hiking with me! I know of some great trails around here, and you would love them."

Yes! I didn't need to think about it. The answer was just 'yes'. I loved hiking, and Daddy and I had climbed Mount Washington together. My father was always happiest when he was outdoors, simply enjoying himself. Then all his impatience and anger seemed to melt away.

"Let's do it!"

We planned to hike the following weekend, and it was a beautiful fall Saturday when Kevin and I met at his house. Even though we hadn't seen each other since the summer, I felt comfortable with him immediately. I felt that he and I had an even stronger connection since Randy's threats. Kevin and I were fellow soldiers in the most distressing war of my life.

I locked my car and we took off in his truck. He played some country music and we sang along. He was such a warm person he made me feel cherished.

We hiked for hours, tramping through the woods, and I could feel my misery lifting with every step. Autumn was my favorite season. I had always seen the fall as a time of new beginnings. The hiking trails lined in the colors of orange, red and yellow reminded me of walking to school and earning stickers on my schoolwork.

I confided to him that if I hadn't been married, I would have been very interested in having a relationship with him. He smiled and revealed that he had the same feelings towards me. I basked in the pleasure of being wanted and desired. We laughed together when we bumped into people who thought we were a couple, and I recognized it was the first time I actually laughed in months. I told him all the details of the past months and for the first time I felt hope for my future and had faith that time would tell me what to do.

Driving back to his house at the end of the day, I looked at him with the same admiration that I had when I first met him.

"You know, I really appreciate you being here for me, even with Randy threatening you."

I let my shoulders relax against the back of the seat as he drove.

"I really enjoyed seeing you Julia and it seemed like you could do with a friend!"

He laughed and I smiled as he pulled into his driveway. My car was parked straight in front of us but there was something odd about it. It seemed to be leaning to one side. I tilted my head, thinking I must have left it on an uneven patch of ground. Then I saw the wheels.

"My tires are flat! It looks like three of them. Three of my tires are flat!"

I thought back to my drive over to Kevin's. I hadn't hit any potholes. Maybe there were some nails in the road. Or maybe…. "Oh my God."

"What? What is it," Kevin asked.

"Is there glass in your driveway?"

"What? No? At least I don't think so?"

It was beginning to make horrible sense to me. Kevin got out and inspected my car.

"They're slashed." He pointed to the cut marks on the tire.

"What do you mean?"

"I mean someone took a knife and stabbed your tires. Come over here and see it for yourself." I was already jumping out of the truck.

"See the cut?" He pointed to a hole in the tire about half an inch long. "That's from a knife, or another very sharp object."

"Are you absolutely sure?" I squinted my eyes at the cut, but he was correct. It looked like a very straight and clean incision across the side of the tire.

Kevin looked at me squarely.

"Julia, I know you know this is not from you driving over something. It was done with a knife, and it was probably Randy."

I started seeing my surroundings as if it was all background, unable to focus on anything. I could hear words coming out of Kevin's mouth but I couldn't understand any of them. I heard only "Randy", "Police", "Dangerous" and "Safety".

"You really think Randy did this?" I asked weakly.

"Don't you?"

I felt myself nod slowly, but it really was too frightening to contemplate. "Do you think he is still here somewhere?"

"I am calling the police, this needs to be reported."

"The police? But how can we prove anything. What if it wasn't him? He wouldn't have done this! He doesn't walk around with knives!" For the first time in a month, I found myself giving Randy the benefit of the doubt.

"Well, I think that he did this time," Kevin responded, while looking around the yard to see if anything else was disturbed. He headed into the house to make the phone call, while I stayed outside feeling exposed and vulnerable. How had he known? Surely my mother would not have been foolish enough to tell him where I was spending the day.

I wondered if he had been following me all this time.

It wasn't long before a police car pulled into the driveway right behind my vehicle. They had come in minutes. They must have thought it was serious. The officer calmly got out.

"Hello Ma'am." He looked at my car and slowly walked over to the tire on the driver's side."

Kevin came out of the house at that moment and provided a brief summary of where we had been and what we had returned home to. He told the officer he believed my ex-husband was responsible. The officer studied us both, then said to me: "Do you know of anyone else who would have wanted to do this to you Ma'am?"

"I have no idea! I have never been in this situation. This isn't what happens in my life. Holy shit!" My voice was becoming louder and faster.

"It's okay Ma'am. We'll get this reported and make sure you can get home safe. Do you have Triple A or a way of getting the vehicle someplace to get some new tires?"

"I can have it towed to Sears and see if they can do it soon."

I felt my body start to quiver and I knew I was close to tears. I closed my eyes but my mind became a frightening theater as I visualized my husband pulling into Kevin's driveway, probably turning his car far too fast, climbing out with the knife in his hand, then swinging it above his head before thrusting it into the thick rubber. And then doing that again and again.

What kind of knife would he have used, I wondered? Where did he even get a knife? Had he casually stopped in a hunting store and bought a knife to use as a weapon? Did he intend to slash the tires or would he have done something else if Kevin and I had been there? Stabbed us like he had stabbed the tires. The questions swirled in my head and I just got more panicky.

I realized I was holding my breath.

I was sure that it wasn't the car he was after. It was me. These stab wounds were meant for me. My heart rate was pounding like a steam train as I looked wildly around Kevin's yard. The police officer was still talking to Kevin. I ran to the end of the driveway and looked up and down the street, but I saw nobody. As the gentle autumn wind blew falling leaves around our ankles, I felt a cold chill despite the warm sun. Randy was a very dangerous person and I had probably seen only the tip of the iceberg.

"Ma'am." The police officer brought me back to the present moment. "After what has happened here today I would recommend that you get a restraining order to keep your ex-husband away from you." So he knew I was in danger too, I thought.

I took the police officer's card and a case number with numb fingers.

I knew I should probably leave straight away, to protect Kevin, but the car was not drivable and I was really in no fit state to make my own way home. He took me inside and settled me on the couch. I lay down in a fetal position as he tried to calm my fears by telling me quietly that everything would be okay. I wasn't so sure of that but hearing it said by someone in such a soothing manner, I almost believed it.

Triple A came and took the car away. I called my mother to tell her what had happened and that I was spending the night at Kevin's. She didn't express any shock, or any concern for my well-being. It was obvious she was more worried that I was spending the night at another man's house.

She delivered her words slowly: "Well, what were you doing over there? You're not coming home?"

"It doesn't matter what I was doing. He slashed the tires on my car! That's not okay. He took a knife and came onto Kevin's property and destroyed my tires," I said angrily.

"What are you going to do?" She asked the question in the same voice I would expect to hear if I had told her I run out of gas on the side of the road.

"I don't know. Mummy. I don't know." I knew she was asking how I intended to get home, but I was referring to my entire life. How was I going to get out of my marriage to Randy without being harmed? "I think I need to call the Morettis. They need to know about this in case he's gone over there while flipping out. He blames them, you know!"

"Well, they shouldn't be getting involved. This is between the two of you. No one should be getting involved. You have to work this out with Randy."

"Mummy, maybe I need someone to be involved, to help me. The Morettis protected me, and I need to protect them as well. Randy stalked me with a knife, and then became violent with a knife. You want me to work this out with him? I really don't think there's anything to work out."

"Okay, well, do what you need to do, honey."

Her sudden detachment surprised me. While not overtly acknowledging what had happened, maybe she was finally resigning herself to the fact that my marriage was over. Or maybe she was just burnt out from all the drama.

I hung up and called the Morettis. Anna's response was more expected. "Julia, you need to get a protective order. This is crazy behavior. He is not safe. If you need someone to go to court with you, I will come. You need to keep yourself safe."

"I know, Anna, the cop said the same thing. I will, I promise." Kevin opened a beer and handed it to me.

"Here, you need it. Want a glass?"

I declined the glass but gladly accepted the bottle. I didn't drink normally but I needed something to help me forget about the day. As one beer turned into two, the alcohol finally started to soothe my frazzled nerves. I melted into the corner of his couch and decided that I would try to appreciate having the evening away from my parents and with the only guy that I really wanted to be with. Kevin ran into another room and came out smiling holding a photo album.

"I want to show you some pictures!" he exclaimed as he sat down, pulled up a footstool and motioned to me to put my feet up with his. I gladly obeyed. We nestled together as he flipped through pages of photos, showing me pictures of summer camp, recent vacations and family gatherings. As we talked about his loved ones and childhood, I told him about mine. Our bond grew stronger as the red line for my marriage became a gray area.

"It's too bad I'm married," I said.

He winked at me. "Well, maybe someday!"

We finished the night by watching a movie and I feel asleep on the sofa.

The following day, Kevin was just as friendly and sweet to me. I needed a solid team of friends and he was proving to me that he would be one of them.

I arrived back at my parents' house the next day. As soon as I stepped into the living room, my mother ran to me like Edith Bunker welcoming Archie home from work in 'All in the Family'.

My mother told me that Randy had called and he wanted to discuss health insurance with me. It seemed so incongruous, given the circumstances, that I almost laughed. However, for the few months prior to our planned Florida move I had been on Randy's health and automobile insurance, and my mother said he wanted to know what my plans were for the future.

On the drive back to my parents' house, I had half convinced myself that it wasn't Randy who had slashed my tires. Now here he was wanting to discuss something as mundane as insurance. I decided to call him. He couldn't hurt me here. I went into a spare bedroom for some privacy.

"Julia?" He sounded shocked as he said my name. I assumed he hadn't expected me to respond.

"Yep, what's up?" I made sure to act as casually as possible. I heard him take a deep breath in and then let it out.

"Well, it's just I have you on my insurance since getting my old job back. I don't want to take you off it if there's a chance of us getting back together again. And then I know you are also on my auto insurance...." His voice trailed off. "This so sad, I love you so much."

But this time the 'nice Randy' act didn't work on me. We had been here before.

"Randy, do what you want," I said sharply. "I am sure I won't get cancer or any major disease soon, and I'll have a job in the near future, so you can just do what you want."

I was no longer afraid of him. This Randy had not slashed my tires, but his alter ego certainly could have.

Although I was pretty convinced it was him, there was a tiny niggling doubt in my mind as he continued talking in a very even, rational way. Could I have it wrong? Could Kevin have had an upset ex-girlfriend who had seen us driving away? My mother was always telling me that I was being ridiculous. I contemplated just asking him outright, but something stopped me.

"Okay, I'll take you off both insurance plans. That's all I wanted to know. Bye, Julia. I do miss you." His voice was the sweet, loving voice that I always longed to hear.

"Bye," I said. If he had slashed the tires, he must have wondered why I was acting so calmly. The thought of wrong footing him made me feel powerful.

The next morning at 8:00 AM, I was still in bed when I heard the phone ringing.

I heard my mother say: "I'll get her!" And then she shouted: "Julia! Are you awake, it's Randy!"

She sounded happy to hear him on the phone. She would never change. For her, everything was forgivable, even mental and physical abuse. She was the epitome of the 'little woman' controlled by her man. But not me.

I watched the same dynamics between my parents now as I did in my childhood. My father would degrade her and call her an idiot, and my mother would tear up and go into another room and work. Sometimes, she would distract herself by a sewing project, or she might wash piles of dishes by hand. This was my role model of a "happy marriage".

"I'll pick up the phone from the other room!" I hollered back.

"Hi Julia." He was using the same voice he had used the day before. Then he started crying.

"I've done a terrible, terrible thing. I have been having a horrible time. I am not doing well at all, Julia." After a gasp for air, he continued. "I am falling apart. I had such an awful weekend."

If I felt any sympathy for him, the next thing he said eliminated it.

"How did you get home yesterday?"

Then I knew. He had done it. His sly question was proof. A chill ran through me, but I was interested to see how he would admit it.

"I drove." My curt answer was intentionally short.

"Drove your car?"

He blew his nose, and then apologized for the interruption.

"Yes."

The next words emerged slowly: "I don't understand."

"I bought new tires."

My voice was unemotional. There was silence from his end. Then he finally spoke.

"That was me." He broke down again. "I'm sorry. I'm so, so sorry. I just went off the deep end; I couldn't control myself, and when I saw your car there, I just lost it. I am so sorry!"

Somewhere, deep inside of me, despite all that had happened, I did feel sorry for him. Whenever he realized the error of his ways, and apologized so sincerely, I always felt sorry for him. I used to berate myself for being taken in by his tears. But it was obvious Randy was a tormented soul, who was indeed not in control of his actions.

My mind went back to when I had once felt love for him. I remembered the tears in his eyes at our wedding.

"What were you thinking?" I asked softly, without recrimination.

"I don't know. I just don't know what happened to me. I am so sorry. I will pay you back for the tires. Please tell Kevin I apologize. I should never have gone to his house!"

"No, you should not have," I confirmed. "I reported what happened to the police and I told them I suspected you."

"What?" He gasped.

"It's okay, I won't press charges."

I knew I was being led by my heart, and not my head, but I had promised to love him for life, and I hadn't. I felt guilty and sad. Deep down I also felt as if I was to blame in some way. He had come back from Florida to collect me, but I had refused to go with him. It was me who had put the wall up, not him. Randy had always said that my behavior was the problem. I wondered whether he was right. My mother certainly believed I wasn't being a dutiful wife.

We ended the conversation with both of us in tears. He reiterated how much he loved me and I responded with "Okay". I couldn't manage anything more. Nothing was clear to me anymore. My mind questioned what love was; who really loved me and who didn't.

The situation between Randy and myself appeared to be draining my mother. Her shoulders were constantly slumped and her face was pale. I was just as concerned for her as I was for myself. Over breakfast one morning she brought up the idea of counseling.

"Honey, I know you are very confused, and I know Randy wants to go to counseling with you, so why don't you at least do that? Why don't you call a therapist, one that you both agree on, and talk to them about the best thing to do?"

"No..." I started to speak.

"Julia, do you have to be like this? This is your husband. You married him and he is hurting. Because of you."

Frustration erupted from me.

"Mother! I won't go with him. But I will go by myself."

I saw the muscles in her face relax.

"That sounds better than doing nothing."

I told myself that at least for the short term, my mother might now get some sleep.

Two weeks later, I was sitting in the waiting room at the Mountainside Mental Health Center, waiting to see a counselor, feeling hopeful that this person might be able to take a good, objective, look at my life and tell me what my best move might be.

As I sat there, I remembered the visit to the family counselor with my parents. I had been equally hopeful then. But this time I would be able to talk for myself and demand a professional response.

"Hello Julia, come in and have a seat. My name is Carla."

Carla smiled at me, her face framed by blond French braids. I smiled back as I ran my hand over my own hair, which was held down with bobby pins. It had been six months since my last haircut. With no money and no motivation, my hair took a backseat. Everything took a backseat.

"Tell me a little bit about you. I see from your intake questionnaire that you are separated."

And with that I started crying; deep, racking, sobs. It was as if my body had seen a green light and started emptying all my pent up emotions into the space between us. I was hardly taking a breath between sentences as I poured out all the events of the previous two months.

"Do you know what emotional abuse is Julia?" Carla asked, eventually.

"Oh no. You don't understand. I'm not abused. He has never hit me!"

"You're saying that you have not been physically abused." She paused for a moment, then went on. "I understand that he hasn't hit you, but emotional abuse is just as damaging, and it sounds like that is exactly what you have been subjected to. Let's talk about that."

Carla described the cycle of control; how one partner will try to put the other one down; try to make them feel bad about themselves. She explained that emotional abuse can range from name calling to playing mind games; embarrassing the other partner and making them feel guilty. As she went on, I realized that I could recall dozens of examples of each of these behaviors. In my mind's eye I saw the incidents written out like a grocery list. Randy had constantly told me I would never find someone better than him; that I was not good enough because I didn't wear make-up or have permed hair, and that I didn't wear clothes that were tight enough for his liking. I remembered him telling my parents, the minister of my church and my friends what I had written in my journal.

When I had refused to go back to him, he had said he was contemplating suicide. He always accused me of causing the problems between us, and making him act a certain way.

In his perspective, my actions caused his disrespectful and violent threats and his temper tantrums. Yes, it did seem like emotional abuse. I was learning a lot.

"Julia, I want to show you something; a diagram that I believe might be helpful to you." Carla pulled out a pad of paper and drew a picture of an upside down triangle on it. She proceeded to label each angle within the triangle; the upper left angle was labeled "Persecutor", the upper right angle was labeled "Rescuer", and the angle at the bottom was labeled "Victim".

"From everything that you have told me, this seems to look like your and Randy's life. Sometimes he's the persecutor and you're the victim; other times, he may be the victim and you are the rescuer. And still other times, you are the persecutor and he's the victim. Basically, you are both playing all the roles."

"I see." I whispered, almost to myself. "I think you are right, Carla, and it's been that way the entire time we have been together."

"Do you know where you want to be in this triangle?" Carla raised her eyebrows. I thought about the different options. None of them seemed that appealing to me.

"Out here!" Carla exclaimed, and she used her pen to point at a spot on the paper about six inches away from the triangle. "You want to be outside of the triangle completely. You do not want to be involved in this at all."

"You're right Carla. It's gone beyond the point of crazy." I shook my head slowly.

"And your friends who advised you to get the restraining order? Listen to them. Go get the restraining order and keep yourself safe." With those words, we ended the session, and I left her office that day with a lot to think about.

CHAPTER 11
RESPECT

"Every good relationship, especially marriage, is based on respect. If it's not

based on respect, nothing that appears to be good will last very long."

— **Amy Grant,** AMERICAN SONGWRITER AND PERFORMER

I wish I could say that I immediately took the advice of the police, Kevin, the Moretti's and Carla and filed a restraining order. But that's not what happened. The reality is I didn't do anything initially. I didn't press charges and I didn't file a restraining order. It just didn't seem right.

I did go to see the Morettis. I hadn't seen them for a couple of months so it was nice to speak face to face again, and they understood Randy even better than I did. While I was not taking precautions, Tony said he was. He and Anna had told their children never to accept a ride home from school with Randy. Tony then pointed out of the window to a large white shade hanging from the roof.

"Julia, do you see those lights on the corner of the house?" I leaned forward.

"Oh yes, those are new. They look great!" I nodded and smiled.

"I didn't get them for their looks." He shook his head. "Those lights are on every side of the house. They turn on when there is any motion at all outside. I've installed them to protect us from Randy."

I was shocked. "You are that worried about him?"

"Yes," Tony nodded. "And so should you be."

It was so hard to believe that Randy would actually do anything to hurt them, or me.

"I also got Anna a very loud personal alarm," he continued. At that point, a screeching sound came from the kitchen. I jumped up and looked around before I realized what it was. Anna walked in holding the small plastic device, smiling.

"You really need to do something to protect yourself," Tony said again. "I know, I know." I closed my eyes and rubbed my forehead. I thought about not only my own safety, but Kevin's as well. I had visited him a few more times since the initial hike, and during the last visit he had told me that he slept with a loaded gun: "Just in case Randy decides to make another visit" were his words. Knowing that my drama was causing other people to fear for their safety made me even more depressed.

I realized, if I wanted to be really honest with myself, that I wasn't getting the restraining order because I was afraid of Randy's reaction. But as I left the Moretti's house that night I promised them I would.

Walking into the house, I went straight to the phone book and picked up the receiver hanging on the dining room wall to call the police department .

My mother, came out from the kitchen holding a dish cloth.

"What are you doing honey?" She looked at me with worried eyes.

"I am finding out how to get a restraining order, and please do not tell me not to," I implored.

"Those Moretti's, they are making you so suspicious. Now be reasonable. We just want you to be reasonable." She included my father in her statement, shaking her head and closing her eyes. I told her the counselor had advised me to do it as well and I was now going forward with it. I would not be derailed this time.

I called Kevin to let him know too, and unlike my mother, he was in complete agreement that a protective order was needed.

The following week, I went to the police station and filled out a form attached to three carbon copies labeled: "Request for Domestic Violence Restraining Order".

Sitting in the public seating area, I looked around me and worried that someone might think I had done something illegal. I was not someone who normally frequented police stations. I took a blue pen from my purse and looked at the form.

Name of Person Asking for Protection and Address? I wrote down my name with my hyphenated last name and the house address belonging to my parents. I was so embarrassed at my obvious failure at marriage and having to state that I had moved back to my parents' house.

Name of Lawyer? Lawyer! I thought only criminals needed lawyers! I just wrote "none".

Person from Whom Protection is sought and relationship to you: Husband – Randy Castleton. I wrote his name out slowly. My heart sank as I thought about the last time I had filled out such an official form, for our wedding license. I thought of us hugging at our wedding and the dreams we had had for our future. Don't think about that, I told myself. Think about the slashed tires, the threats and the hurt that he has caused. Think about the fact that your friends are afraid of this guy. Think about the fact that even he says he cannot control himself.

Description of Harassment: That one was easy. He slashed three tires on my car after stalking me. I liked the black and white nature of that answer. Nobody could argue with it. It was not a gray area like the rest of my marriage.

After submitting the form, I was provided with a temporary restraining order, as well as a court hearing date for two weeks later, to establish the permanent order. I saw the rest of the process as just administrative. I needed to go through the motions. I told myself that on the date of the hearing, I would dress to the nines, I would be extremely respectful to the judge and I would show them that I was not one of their normal cases; not their normal clientele. I was above all this.

Later that night, Randy called the house and my mother answered the phone. She handed it to me. I chose not to tell him about the restraining order and impending court date. I didn't want to deal with his reaction at that moment.

"What do you want?" I asked him as I rolled my eyes at my mother.

"I just want to tell you, I was talking to your brother, Rob and..." I didn't give him a chance to finish his sentence.

"Why were you talking to my brother? You've never been close to my brother."

"I just wanted to get his opinion." His voice was as soft and gentle as Mr. Rogers.

"Really?" By this point, he had already reached out to my parents, my older sister, Debra and now Rob to explain to them how unreasonable he thought I was being.

"Rob told me that he and his wife are expecting a baby next summer, and I was thinking, perhaps you and I, we can get back together and have a baby. I want to have a baby with you, Julia."

"A baby?" I was astounded.

His calm voice continued. "I have taken the high road throughout all of this, Julia. No matter what you did to me, I have always been willing to take you back. I am doing everything in my power to save our relationship."

"No, Randy, no baby and I disagree with you on that 'high road' that you seem to believe you have taken."

Within ten seconds, the gentle Mr. Roger's voice flipped to the loud angry voice, just like my father's. "Then I am fucking filing for divorce! You put no effort into this. I feel like I'm the only one that cares about this marriage!"

"Okay, that's fine. You get a lawyer, I will get one too. I can't keep up with this crap. I can't keep up with the back and forth. You are one extreme or the other. One minute you love me, the next minute, you hate me, and it's continuously been that way for months now, if not years!"

For the following two weeks, I did not hear from him. I assumed he had been informed of the court date and knew not to contact me.

Randy didn't show up on the day of the hearing. I wondered if he was advised not to. It never occurred to me that someone would simply not show up for court. As a result, the judge didn't ask me anything. I was automatically awarded the protective order.

I was on my way out of the courtroom when a friendly-looking woman handed me a business card and a brochure. I thanked her then looked down to read it. The title was: " Safe Haven House : a fully funded protected environment for those impacted by domestic violence."

They think I'm a victim of domestic violence, I thought. But I don't have black eyes. I felt like a fraud. Randy just said things he didn't really mean.

But then I thought about the true crime books I had read in the last several years. Every murderer had the same personality traits as Randy; the insecurity, the manipulation and the arrogance. The 'Safe Haven House' woman was probably just trying to get to me before it was too late. Maybe I was a typical client after all, and I was not "above" all this. I could die as easily as anyone else.

I no longer had any love for this man. Where did it go? Did it slink its way out of the back door when no one was looking, during the initial stages of the verbal and emotional abuse? Or did it wait around and escape my soul while Randy was on his way to Florida, or when he was stalking me with the knife? Or did it slip away a little every time a friend of mine chose to put their own life and safety at risk to make sure I was safe?

It's possible that the love didn't escape. It simply died. It lost its strength a little at a time, like a dying flame in a fire pit. One percent gone for each time he told me I messed everything up (when I knew I hadn't); one percent for each time he told me how lucky I was to have him, another one percent gone for every conversation he had with my loved ones, manipulating them to side with him (and succeeding). With enough one percents gone, the marriage was doomed.

I later found out that when Randy was served the permanent restraining order by the police officers, he was so angry he had ripped up every picture in our wedding album and threw the destroyed album across the room.

How would his violence have ended? Inside I knew, if I had stayed, it would have ended in my death.

He crushed his wedding band in a rage. I knew that would eventually have been my skull.

He had thrown things around the room on multiple occasions. I knew that would eventually have been my torso.

He slit the tires on my car; it could easily have been my throat.

I sat down and wrote him a letter at the same dining room table I had used in high school. Ten years, and this is where I end up, I thought. I was disgusted with myself. Taking a deep breath, I looked up from the paragraphs I had just written explaining why I didn't want our marriage any more, as my mother moved from the kitchen sink, where she had been scrubbing dishes, to the basket of clothes that needed folding.

"Mummy, I can't believe how much you work. Look at yourself. It's 10:30 at night!" I pointed to the clock; the same clock that was there also ten years prior, further reminding me of my stalemate position in life.

"This isn't work!" She flung her hands up in front of the laundry basket. "If you call this work, no wonder you and Randy didn't get along! This is just a part of life!"

I thought about explaining to her that my desire to not perform housekeeping tasks all evening was not the cause of our separation, but it reminded me of Randy's endless mantra: "It's a wife's job to clean and decorate the house in order to provide a home that feels safe for her husband!"

"I work full time and you are home first, so why don't you start creating your own safe environment!" I had screamed back at the time. But my mother shared his perspective across the board.

"Mother, we are divorcing because he doesn't have any respect for me. He may say he does, but he doesn't."

"Divorcing?" her voice cracked.

"Yes, let me read to you what I am summarizing for him, so he can refer to it in the future, whenever he wonders why we split up."

My mother's audible sigh made me wonder if she would actually listen to me.

I grabbed the notebook.

"Okay, here goes." I looked at my mother to make sure her full attention was on me.

Her auburn colored hair had a dried out look, making her appear even more tired than normal. She frowned as she nodded at me to start.

"Randy, you don't love me. I know this because love to me is respect and you don't respect me." I looked up from the paper and at my mother. She opened her mouth and my whole body clenched knowing she was about to defend Randy. "No, just listen, Mummy," I blurted, and kept going.

"If you respected me, you wouldn't go through my journals and notebooks looking for personal items because of your lack of trust. If you respected me, you wouldn't have advertised what I wrote in my journal to my family and our friends, and say "Boy! She's 28 years old!" as if my actions were due to immaturity. If you respected me, you wouldn't tell Tony that you had the upper hand and you were 'getting laid on Friday night'. If you respected me, you wouldn't call my mother on your way to Florida saying: 'I'm divorcing your daughter, now she can chase all the men she wants.' And that's not even beginning to mention all the violence in our relationship."

I looked at my mother.

"Honey, he's doing the best that he can!"

"I know Mother, that is the problem. This is his best. And if this is his best, and I do believe it is, I would hate to see his worst."

I saw the tears well up in her eyes as she slowly set down the white T-shirt she was folding.

"Mother, listen. He can't control himself. He takes no responsibility for anything he's done except in false apologies, which he recants minutes later. His violence is becoming worse. I can't believe you want me to go back to that! He is going to kill someone someday. You will be thankful it's not me!"

I pictured the news story coming across the television screen, and the headlines in the newspaper. "Man Kills Wife in Domestic Dispute". I thought of my mother saying: "Oh Julia! Oh my God, I am so glad you left him!" I saw her expressing the love and emotion for me that she rarely chose to show.

But now she closed her eyes and shook her head slowly. "Give him another chance, Julia. This entire thing is up to you, you're the one deciding the future here. Don't you want your marriage to work out?"

I couldn't understand why she thought I had so much power over this situation, as if something so big could be controlled by just me. I remembered a scene, sixteen years earlier; a similar conversation in the same room. But that time it was her marriage we were discussing. Through my twelve-year old screams, after watching my father smack my sister across the face, I had begged my mother to tell me why she stayed with my father,

"Look at him!" I screeched at her. "Why don't you divorce him. You should just divorce him!"

"By God!" she hollered back. "If we ever do get a divorce, it will be because of you children!"

"Because of us children?" I had retorted, feeling a need to defend not only myself, but Jennifer as well. "You think we caused this?"

"Well, you don't see me getting him going, do you? You kids don't know when to keep your mouths shut."

She broke down and cried then, just as she was breaking down now. It occurred to me that in her mind, I would have been responsible for making her marriage come apart then, just as I was responsible for making my own marriage come apart now.

I hated the idea of hurting my mother, but I hated the idea of going back to my marriage even more.

"I have given him multiple chances, Mummy. He keeps making things worse. Every time I think it can't get worse, it does." How could I get this across to her? I'd tried every explanation I could think of.

My mother reached over to a pile of handkerchiefs she had just finished folding and took one to wipe her eyes. As she wiped each eye, she let out a sigh: "Well, honey, we can't get through to you. No one can."

I went to bed shortly after that, knowing I would need to file for divorce without the support of my parents.

I called the law office in a nearby strip mall the following day: "Give me any divorce lawyer that's inexpensive," I told the secretary.

"It depends how complicated the divorce will be," she explained. I assured her that I owned nothing and wanted nothing from him; I simply wanted out. "Just, please, get me out of this," I begged, as if asking for assistance to bail me out of jail.

While filling out the divorce papers I felt no more emotional than when I filled out job applications.

Two days later, Legal Remedies, LLC proved to me that they process divorces more efficiently than the Division of Motor Vehicles processes car registrations. I was in and out of their office within one hour. The Legal Aid advisor at the clinic explained to me that Randy's lawyer would need to obtain information, and Randy would need to sign the documentation as well. I wondered what he might object to, knowing he would probably do everything he could to delay, in the hope of buying time to convince me to go back to him.

Some friends had told me, months earlier, that it was a good thing that this happened before we bought a house or had children. There is nothing "good" about this, I thought. How can anyone have such a lack of understanding? But now, I understood. I didn't want to fight over property, money, and certainly not custody of children. I just wanted out.

I felt the most pain for the upset that I was inflicting on my parents. There were too many episodes my parents had not been witness to and they truly didn't understand. Although I suspected my dad did. My heart felt broken as I was systematically letting go of my dream, of a lifetime marriage. It had been, just that; merely a dream.

The next day I arrived home from a substitute teaching assignment to find another letter on my bed. It had my name on it and the words: "My last letter on this case – I write it better than I can talk it". I recognized my mother's difficult to read handwriting.

Dear Julia,

A lot of thoughts have been passing by me – since this whole episode has been coming down to the wire. I've been having some extra serious thoughts that I have to share with you – these are what we called "wishes" back along.

I respect all the anger you have been holding but ever since you made that big move of filing D – that really shook me. After you told me what you wrote to Randy about all the "respects" he never had (which all seemed true), I got to thinking - The man never was brought up to show "respect" and I don't think that was ever in his vocabulary in his upbringing. It's hard to punish someone for something they know nothing about. In this trial, he has been beaten. You won the battle and he knows – you filed and is "tired of arguing". But Julia – Even though you've proved your point over and over again – Don't give him the death penalty. I guess what I am getting at why not try and let him prove himself – maybe a second and a half chance , you would have nothing to lose. Live in your own "quarters", come and go, you could still be "family" with the pups, etc. Keep your car on his and health insurance (since you have none). Make sense to me!

Then in time, if it seems to work, take it from there onward or if it doesn't go anywhere, you will still have your own place, a job and your own financing.

No – he has not done any "crying to me" so he doesn't know how I feel about it. These are my thoughts. If you put your best foot forward, you will not be sorry. You would be much more happier with yourself than you would if you went ahead with the D.

Discuss it with sincerity with Jennifer. Randy has been to hell and back or you have with it all and all it's doing is tearing you both to pieces (not saying what it's done for someone who loves you both and your little family)

If this is all crap to you, that's ok too. I will still stand behind you (+ Dad too) – it might not be my choice, what we want for you but your dad and I want you to be happy in whatever you do. If you see this is not possible then do one thing, go to see him once before the D and see it face to face.

We love you or we wouldn't be sick over it all as we are –

Love you,
Mom

If I just put my "best foot forward" I will not be sorry. For some reason, those words stabbed me like a knife. My mother had given Randy so much credit for trying his best but she didn't have the same belief in my efforts. In her heart, I hadn't tried my best yet; I hadn't given it my all.

She couldn't even write out the word divorce. I wanted to take her pain away but at what cost? In tears, I called my sister, Jennifer, who continued her unwavering support.

"Julia, you are doing the right thing. Go forward with the divorce. Don't you see? You are just living chapter one of a Danielle Steel novel. This is just chapter one. This is just the little backstory, before your real life begins."

"Did he contact you too? Did you know he contacted Rob?" I stared at the floor, wishing I could see my sister in person.

"Oh – he tried, I just blew him off," Jennifer assured me. "He can only get away with that shit with Rob because Rob wants so much to be liked, and making you the bad guy makes them feel like a team; you know, having a common enemy."

I smiled to myself and was thankful for her support. She was always so insightful. I was thankful too that Randy hadn't been able to pull her into his web, as he had my parents and my oldest brother. For a while now, I'd had minimal contact with all my siblings as my family began drifting apart; a familial separation that would become increasingly worse over the following 20 years. In the future, I would come to understand that the separation within my family, as well as my choice of marriage partner, was a direct result of being brought up in an abusive household.

"Just chapter one. Ah Jennifer. Well, I certainly hope this book gets better!" I giggled through my tears.

"It will, Julia, it definitely will – send the jerk on his way!"

"Got It!" I responded, and we ended the phone call on an optimistic note, if a little forced from my end.

Chapter one turned into chapter two as my job search finally yielded a new role. I was offered a job teaching accounting and basic math to high school students, and I was thrilled. It also meant I would have health, dental and auto insurance, removing some of my mother's reasons for why I should stay with Randy. I could now join a health club, and start thinking about moving out of my parent's house. Ironically, as the cooler air of late fall and the days of less sunlight encroached upon New England, my world began to look a little brighter.

The move to my own apartment happened faster that I had planned. My siblings arrived home for Thanksgiving and the same family dynamics from childhood reemerged. Brian flew in from out of state and he and I sat on the couch and love seat, covered with worn homemade olive slipcovers, and talked. The old high school pictures of us were still in the frames on the top of the television. It felt like we had gone back a decade. Because he had flown home, I offered him my car to go to a movie with a friend.

"It's nothing fancy, but it'll get you guys there and back!"

Before Brian had a chance to respond, my father came in from the dining room and interjected: "No one asked to use your goddam car, Julia. He isn't interested." There was no need for the outburst.

"Daddy, I'm offering it to them to be nice. Why do you have to be so unpleasant?"

My mother looked at me disgustedly. "Stop the fighting!" she begged, just as she had in my childhood.

"He doesn't need to be a jerk!" I shouted to my mother, as she gathered her sewing materials to make her exit from the room.

"Oh, so I'm the jerk? I'm the only one around here doing any work, supporting everyone, and I'm the jerk?" My father raised his arms in the air indicating he'd had enough.

"Not for long, Daddy." I reached over for the newspaper. "That's made up my mind. I'm moving out." I grabbed the phone and started making phone calls from the newspaper apartment listings.

"No, Julia! You don't need to do that!" My mother pleaded.

"I do need to Mummy. I have a job now and I can't put up with this crap like you can; I have to get out of here!"

Jennifer and I went for a walk to get away from the house. Brian took my car to escape, and my parents were left wondering what had happened. Later that day Jennifer found a bottle of vodka in the shower. She told my mother who told her to mind her own business. We realized she would always protect our father and there was nothing we could do about it.

CHAPTER 12
THE FINAL STRAW

"There is always a final straw, but it's not any worse than the dozens of straws

that came before. They were the same. You just finally learned the lesson that

you are more than what you settled for."

—

Stephanie Bennett-Henry, CANADIAN POET AND AUTHOR.

It was the Friday night before Christmas when I decided to explain the details of my upcoming move to my parents.

Although the apartment search had been prompted by negative circumstances, I was excited to make the change, and by the thought of living independently. I had found a two-bedroom apartment for a good price in a large complex, available almost imme-diately . My biggest issue was that I still had minimal funds to spend on household furnishings and supplies. I needed everything from silverware to a living room couch and a bed.

My mother and father and I sat in the same living room where our family celebrated every Christmas. We all stared at the sweet smelling pine tree and I was mesmerized by the red and green blinking lights. As fresh snow fell, outside the large picture window behind it, one might have mistaken the scene for a Norman Rockwell painting. But this wasn't a Christmas that I would remember fondly. There had been very few of those. From my pre-teenage to young adult years, every holiday meant new family fights. Ev-ery holiday season, my mother would repeat many times as we approached Christmas Day: "I just want to get through this holiday. Just get me through it."

I think it was half a statement to herself and half a prayer to God. One year my oldest sister Debra came to Christmas dinner with a story about a conversation she had with her friends.

Debra told us how she and her fellow band members were talking about what family members wanted for Christmas,

"My mother said she just wants peace!" Debra told her friends.

One friend responded: "Oh, world peace! Isn't that nice that your mother would think that way during the holiday season."

"No, not world peace," Debra corrected them. "Peace in our house. She just wants peace in our house. She wants a break from all the fights. There are fights in my house every day."

"Oh," was the response from the friend. I believe Debra single-handedly put a stop to the holiday cheer with that conversation.

For me, this Christmas season was another first. Like having a death in the family, I had made peace with the fact that for the upcoming 365 days, every holiday would be a first, without Randy. I had survived the first Thanksgiving, despite the family blowup, and now I needed to survive Christmas.

I looked out of the window at the falling snow, and then at my mother, who was also staring at the tree. She had convinced me, since I'd received her last letter, to call my lawyer and put the divorce on hold. Randy had been claiming he was going to Co-dependent Anonymous meetings and getting the help that he needed to calm his emotional rages. He had showed some empathy when I said I missed the dogs. He brought them over to my parent's house every couple weeks so I could have them for the weekend. Every time he was kind, every time he acted normally, every time he turned up on my parents' doorstep with the dogs, I wavered just a little bit. I suppose that was normal but it made me feel weak. It always started my marriage vows playing on a loop in my head.

To make my mother happy I agreed to attending one counseling session with Randy, with the possibility of going to a second depending on how things went. Then, to show that I was putting in some effort, I forced myself to go to the movies with him too. I refused to hold his hand at the movie theatre though, feeling I was not ready to make any commitment of any kind, and it ended up in a fight. The truth was my heart just wasn't in it anymore. I couldn't stand being with him. I knew then I had made, and was making, the right decision. Now was the time to take back full control of my own life.

"So, my first day in the apartment is officially January 3rd, but the landlord said I can move in early, on the first, if I'd like!" I smiled, raising my eyebrows, looking for equal excitement in their eyes.

"So what are you thinking about taking?" my mother asked dully.

"Well – um, my sleeping bag, my books from college, maybe the 13-inch TV that I used in college. I think that's still around here right?'

"What about the other stuff you'll need?"

"Well, I'll see what I can do with a couple of hundred dollars at Walmart. I think I can get a few dishes, not a whole set, and maybe a few glasses and silverware. I turned to my father. "Can I take a couple of the old fold-out lawn chairs from the basement, the ones that you don't use anymore?"

He looked at me over the top of glasses: "You're going to have fold out lawn chairs in your living room?"

"Yeah, why not?"

"Okay, we'll see what we can do with them." Daddy was great at taking items other people called trash and restoring them, and he enjoyed seeing those items "put to good use" (his words). I would certainly put any items he gave me to good use.

"Great!" I smiled from ear to ear. For the first time in months I looked to my future with optimism. I visualized my work being appreciated each day, learning new skills and receiving a paycheck every two weeks. I visualized my apartment getting a little better every month. I saw myself eventually buying a small table, a couple of real chairs, a bed, and maybe even a couch. I could see the light at the end of the tunnel.

As soon as I moved in, with my car load of things, a week later, I was in love. The fold-out chairs and campground level sleeping arrangements made no difference to me. I was free, and I could spend my time as I wanted, with no one watching over me. No panicking husband, no over-emotional mother and no drinking father. Nobody. It was perfect.

A week later, I returned to my apartment after a day of teaching to find a real couch in my living room; not new, but a real one, plus end tables, a coffee table and a TV stand! I walked into my bedroom and there was a double bed with a nightstand next to it! Daddy!

I could not have been more happy if I had won the lottery. I ran through my 800 square foot apartment looking at each of the new additions. "Oh My God!" I shouted aloud, after checking out a standing lamp in the living room. I gasped again as I saw my books, that had been in cardboard boxes, all lined up on a bookshelf in the bedroom.

In the kitchen there was a note from my father.

"Picked up a few things at 'Happy Homecoming Charities' during my last delivery and thought this might help out." Tears welled in my eyes. Since retiring from his job, my father had volunteered several days a week with a charitable organization helping homeless people become independent. My father would drive to places to pick up donations, and then make deliveries of donated items to people in need. I had no problem being considered "in need". The Julia who saw herself as too good to be in a courtroom was long gone. I appreciated any help provided from anyone with good intentions.

Over the next month, I made it a point to become more active. I ran mid-winter road races, went skiing with friends from college, joined a church and volunteered with 'Habitat for Humanity'. I worked out frequently at my health club and soaked in the hot tub after swimming. I remembered the person I used to be before the drama of living with Randy, and I liked her very much. It was a joy getting to know the old me again. Freedom tasted sweet. I loved going to work every day because my co-workers knew me as only the new me, never having known Randy, or anyone else.

It was after a two day skiing trip that I arrived home to find my phone message machine blinking.

"You have three messages." The digitized voiced told me.

"Julia, this is Randy. Where are you? Call me!" Click. The desperation in his voice was not unfamiliar to me and all I thought was "Here we go again."

I pressed play for the next message.

"Julia, where the hell are you? What the hell are you doing? Did you not come back last night? Call me as soon as you get in. Call me!" Click.

The new Julia whispered in my right ear: "Tell him 'Fuck you' and move on." I looked at the speaker on the answering machine and said, "Fuck You Randy".

Then I noticed the old Julia stepping in, along with my mother's voice in my other ear, and both whispered: "God – he sounds so desperate, so needy, you better do something, help the poor guy!"

But immediately, new Julia took over the conversation in my head. "No, nothing needs to be done for poor Randy. Poor Randy has had a job this whole time, an apartment and every opportunity to make a life for himself. He has simply chosen not to. " I realized I agreed with new Julia as I pressed the button the third time. This message was much louder than the prior ones.

"Julia, where the fuck are you? You're off seeing someone I'm sure! You're seeing Kevin, or is it your college friend, Paul? No I'll bet it's Michael in Colorado, or your supposedly gay friend, Andrew. He's not gay. He's just telling you that to get you in bed! You can screw all the men you want. I don't give a shit. Where the fuck are you? You were out all night weren't you? Don't lie to me. I can't be married to shit like you. I am so sorry I ever fucking married you. That was the worst mistake I ever made in my life. I am calling my lawyer and telling him to step up this divorce. I don't want you anymore. You can go fuck all the men you want!"

I stared at my answering machine. My mind ran through my most recent activities. Work, work, work, work, work, ski, run, ski again and then a girl's night out for drinks. Some of my friends were females and some were males.

I called him back and matched both his volume and his profane choice of words.

"Randy, don't you dare think that you have any say over what I do with my own time. I am an adult. I have my own apartment, I have my own job, I have my own fucking everything. You have zero say over anything. You treat me as if I am a child and you are my father. You and I are done. Where I have been is none of your damn business! You get on with your life and I will get on with mine."

Randy said I didn't know the mistake I was making and followed it up with: "You will never be able to find love like mine again. Never!"

This was the last straw. It wasn't worse than prior fights; it wasn't louder, it wasn't as violent, but it was the last. I no longer felt trapped in any way. I had the freedom to have a normal life and nothing was tying me down to this harmful relationship.

I called Kevin even though I hadn't seen him in a couple months. "Hey, I just want to let you know, Randy's gone off his rocker again. Heads up."

"My neighbors told me they saw a little white car pull into my driveway a few times over the weekend …a white Ford Probe."

"Yep, that's his car," I confirmed.

"I couldn't believe he was still hunting me. I couldn't help but wonder, what did he bring this time? Was it the same knife that he used to stab my tires, or was he ready to up the anti? Was it a gun this time?"

I felt so guilty that Kevin was living with all this worry just because of his friendship with me.

"It really is beginning to get to me Julia, so I have no idea how you are handling it."

"I am so sorry Kevin," I said. "I truly don't think he would ever actually hurt someone." But even as I said it I wondered if I believed it. "I will talk to him and make it clear there is no relationship between us."

I called my lawyer and told him to go forward with the divorce. Maybe Randy just needed finality to let go.

I sat down and wrote Randy my last communication with him.

After listing all the ways he had hurt me, I ended the several page letter with the following:

I can't think of too many people that I would quit my job, quit my church, leave school, and leave all my friends and family behind for, and be willing to support financially and emotionally for four years (even for the rest of my life). I loved you and was willing to do that for you.

I am afraid for my well-being now. I am afraid for my friends and family. I don't feel you are stable emotionally, and it would not be beneficial for me to put myself in a situation where I will be hurt even more.

Randy, I do hope you go to counseling and grow from this experience. I hope that you work on these problems that seem to linger from your past. But, I can't do it with you. I have to put me first in my life. I hope for your sake, and your future relationships, that you work these issues out.

I didn't tell my parents anything. I didn't tell my mother that I had taken the hold off the divorce proceedings. I hoped that my divorce would go through silently. My parents would never have to know when it actually happened. I hoped that eventually I would introduce them to a new boyfriend and my old marriage would just fade away.

CHAPTER 13
THE DIVORCE DECREE

"Not today, not this week, maybe not even this year but one day...... One day your mask will fall and they will see the monster I had to face alone. They will know that I wasn't lying, there really was a demon behind that angelic face. They will know...."

– Karishma R.K aka Phoenix Mode, AUTHOR

I have always felt a spiritual connection with my grandmother with whom I share my middle name. I never met Eloise though. She died 12 years before I was born.

She divorced my unstable, alcoholic grandfather 50 years to the day that I divorced Randy. I sat in my living room, staring at my own divorce decree. It had arrived in the mail the day before and required my signature before it could be finalized by the judge. If only my grandmother had still been alive, she could have given me support and guidance.

Her divorce decree had a more truthful reason than my own. "Extreme Cruelty" it had said on her papers. After hearing the stories of my grandfather's alcoholism and infidelity, he had indeed sounded very cruel. My own reason was "irreconcilable differences", when perhaps I should have sued him for cruelty too. I hadn't wanted to give Randy a reason to disagree with it and refuse the divorce.

I wanted to put the last six years of my life behind me. I was so physically and emotionally exhausted from the fights, the drama, and the going back and forth.

At this point, our communication was in phone calls. Randy had not given up his attempt to exercise power over me.

One minute he would claim to love me, want me back and beg me to forgive him, and the next minute he would explode at me, tell me what a terrible person I was and how much he despised me. The next day, he would want me back again, even after no changes had been made by either one of us. I sat on my living room floor, with my back against the couch, and sadly read the decree

Julia E. Sinclair-Castleton
vs.
Randall C. Castleton

I thought of the happy times. I thought of the late night talks; going out to barbecues and laughing with our friends; running the Boilermaker road races after training so long and hard together for them. I thought of him asking me to marry him in the restaurant, with a special cake in front of us that he had pre-ordered, and I thought of him crying on our wedding day when saying "I do". I pulled out a small, aqua-colored, wedding album. "Our Wedding Memories" was the title. I flipped through the three photos per page, filled with smiles, bridesmaids, and wedding cake; pages that showed me the wedding I wanted, but not the marriage I had.

However, as easily as I remembered the good times, I remembered every insult, every act of violence, and every attempt to control me. I had to admit to myself that I had seen Randy's traits while we were dating, and even just before the wedding, but I had chosen not to make them show stoppers. I remembered him telling me that I was not the ideal wife because my voice was loud and I had opinions. "Good wives aren't like that. Good wives allow their husbands to be in control and are much more passive," he had said.

I recalled him flipping over the dining room table out of anger when I refused to do what he wanted. I still couldn't understand how his personality could turn on a dime, but it did. He was completely unpredictable.

I had learned to deny reality when I didn't want to see it. And when I was forced to see it, I had chosen to just wait and hope for the best. Maybe if I waited long enough, like my mother did, the craziness might stop and maybe things would get better. But they were not better for her. My siblings and I had moved out; my father still drank and my mother just learned to adjust. I could not make the adjustments that she made, or any adjustments that this marriage would require me to make.

After all the conversations and letters from my mother, her begging me to stay in the marriage, I just couldn't do it. I couldn't fake love and I couldn't make my own life miserable.

I feared Randy's violence would progress over time; his rages would escalate even more and, eventually, he would kill. I was sure of it. I didn't want to be the female he was obsessed with when he got to that point.

I turned my attention back to the decree. I looked over the agreed-upon splits; I would take half the credit card debt and my own car, along with the possessions that I brought into the marriage. That was it. I signed the decree. I then put it in an envelope to be sent out the next day. As the tears rolled down my cheeks, I prayed that the universe would lead me in the direction I was supposed to go in the least painful way possible.

The court date was set for three months later. Randy didn't appear.

I asked my lawyer to fill out a form to keep the reporting of the divorce out of the town newspaper. I explained that as I taught in the school district, I didn't want to be the subject of rumors. I was thankful that it wasn't published, so my mother, and her friends, couldn't know.

I found out later though that it didn't matter. As soon as Randy had received notification that we were divorced, he called my mother to say: "It was nice having you as a mother-in-law. I just wanted to say good-bye."

Randy didn't know how to love. He deliberately hurt my mother. His actions were to make himself feel better. My mother kept the call short, saying good-bye and hid her pain.

SECTION 3
MIDDLE AGE

CHAPTER 14
DEATH OF MY FATHER

"Life gives many topics for reflection, but little time"

– www.StatusMind.com

I sat on a dented metal chair, watching my father slowly ebb away in a poor quality nursing home which the local hospital had sent him to. As much trauma as he had put me and my siblings through in our childhood, I remembered the love that he had showed me too.

I remembered hiking; going for morning runs around the neighborhood; him taking us camping, and saving every penny he had to send me and my brothers and sisters to college.

The doctors at the hospital had declared that Daddy's cancer was terminal and they had given up hope. I was suddenly jealous of every person who died quickly in a car accident or from a stroke. He was now paralyzed in bed as the tumor in his back was pressing on his spine. We had only found out about it five weeks before.

I looked at his wristband: "Walter Henry Sinclair" DOB 1/18/31". I realized that one day that was all anyone would know about him. It didn't seem possible that such a larger than life character could just slip away.

The television was on in the corner and I was glad for its distraction, even though I wasn't taking anything in. All I could think about was cancer, pain, fear and death.

I stared out of the window at one small oak tree, standing alone in an open area. The tiny leaves were just beginning to turn from green to bright yellow and orange, reminding us that summertime was coming to an end. I was so thankful that this worst summer of my life was nearly over.

After spending so much of his life outdoors, now my father was ending his days in a small drab room, far away from home. At least he would see his last New Hampshire fall, even if it was only one tree.

"So, there's been a lot of time for thinking," he suddenly said. "You know, your Aunt Mary left home and went to live in Rhode Island without telling anyone where she went." I had heard this story before, but I let my father talk. It filled the time. "You know, I don't think her mother, Betty, ever recovered from her disappearance."

Betty was my step-grandmother; the woman that Grandfather Sinclair had married after my grandmother, Eloise, divorced him for abuse and adultery. He had cheated on my grandmother with Betty, and Mary had been their baby; my father's half-sister.

"She loved Mary so much, possibly too much. I don't think your Aunt Mary thought about the impact that leaving would have on her mother." He grew quiet for a moment and then continued. "Then, Betty died and we couldn't even find your Aunt Mary. We had to get the police involved and they found her eventually and told her that her mother was dead."

I thought of the horror of finding out something so awful that way.

When we were young, Aunt Mary had always been presented as someone bad. If any of us children did something wrong our parents would say: "You'll grow up to be just like your Aunt Mary."

I had always imagined her as this out-of-control rebel. But my father was now speaking about her with an affection I didn't know he had harbored. His sense of loss was tangible.

"Mistakes and regrets…" my father mumbled. He turned his head to look at his tree.

"Well, you certainly don't have the monopoly on mistakes," I sighed. "I should never have married Randy."

My father smiled gently at me, with this new calm I had never seen before.

"You two just didn't get along," he said sadly. Such a simple comment for all the years of pain and heartbreak my husband had put us all through.

For a moment I balked at his acceptance. I had not yet accepted all the screaming, crying, yelling, accusations, stalking, tire slashing and subtle violence. But my father was on his deathbed and I didn't want to upset him. I wondered if this was his way of forgiving me; for the trouble my choice of husband had brought into their lives. 'You just didn't get along.' A simple, blameless statement, drawing a line under the past.

"Well, at least it is all over now."

We both stared out of the window then, as I pondered on all the changes since Randy. I had Ed now, and since meeting him, a fellow teacher, the same year that I had divorced Randy, he had given me five years of stability and happiness. Ed was the opposite of Randy; calm, cool, and easy-going. Seeing me happier than ever, both of my parents adjusted to my new life very well and liked Ed a lot. He popped in and out to keep my father company too.

I was on a break from work and knew I needed to go back to the office, but I felt bad because I didn't want to leave him alone. Just a few more minutes, I thought.

"So, where's your brother, Rob? I haven't seen him in quite a while."

"I don't know." It was obvious that was why he had been thinking about Mary. "Mummy should be by to visit in about an hour, and then Jennifer is coming over tonight," I offered, trying to make up for his eldest son's absence. There was no malice in Rob towards Daddy; he just wasn't the caring type. I could see my father was growing tired so I moved to take my leave. I kissed him on the forehead and tiptoed out. Once I got out to my car, I cried like a baby.

Later that night Jennifer told me my father had asked her about Rob's suicide. We put the comment down to the amount of morphine he was taking, but it showed his mind was preoccupied by his son. I felt I needed to do something to reunite my father and Rob, and Rob's five year-old son, before it was too late, as it had been for Aunt Mary. I wrote him an email. I explained that our dad was in a lot of pain, but comforted by having his family around him, and made it clear that I felt he should be there too.

My mother was not impressed by what I had done. For her there was nothing more important than keeping the peace.

"Why, Julia? Why do you always have to start something?"

"Because it's important. Daddy needs him there."

"If it's not Jennifer causing trouble, it's you. Just leave Rob alone."

I got the impression my mother feared Rob, as much as she feared my father. This weakness felt like a betrayal to me. She would always back down, even if it meant not supporting me, rather than tackling problems head on.

Rob never mentioned the letter to me but he did visit for a couple of hours that weekend, three days before my father passed away. I hoped Rob's rare visit had brought my father some peace. I was glad I had made the move.

The loss of my father hit me like a ton of bricks. I found myself wishing he was around for everything; my house being built, our two new dogs and my wedding to Ed.

But in the years to come, I was thankful that he was not around to witness the breakdown of my family, his family, as the ripple effect of abuse and emotional neglect sent tidal waves through our relationships.

CHAPTER 15
COUNSELING AS ADULTS

"If you want to understand today, you have to search yesterday"

– Pearl S. Buck, AMERICAN WRITER AND NOVELIST

My father had been dead for two years. It had been almost 25 years since our last attempt at family counseling, and the only change over the years was the name of the abuser. Instead of my father being the perpetrator, Rob was now the offender causing waves in our family.

Rob and I had actually grown closer as adults. As we had each maneuvered our way through "real life" after college, we would go out for Chinese food and commiserate about relationships gone bad, or our sporadic successes. But when he got married and had a baby we lost a lot of that closeness. Gradually he detached from us all. My brother Brian had separated by distance rather than emotion, and was now living in California, but happy for us to visit. Rob, however, wasn't open to including his childhood family in his new life.

He had a foul temper, and unlike our father he didn't need any assistance from a bottle to put him in that state. It was obvious he had been as affected by our upbringing as I had. Cruel behavior was his go to state when he felt defensive. When I asked him why he had cut us all off, but me especially, a pulsing vein protruded from his forehead and he said cryptically: "I can't have you involved. I need to keep my marriage together!"

I wondered if contact with his family brought back too many unpleasant memories, and unsettled him. His wife didn't do anything to foster communication either.

After years of attempted reconciliations, and disrespectful, or non-existent, responses, Jennifer and I had written Rob off. I no longer accepted abuse, unlike my mother, and I wasn't prepared to be mistreated, even by my own brother.

I would later learn that Rob and Randy had developed a friendship after my divorce. Perhaps they shared a common bond of dislike of me.

My mother tried very hard to keep in contact with her first-born son. Once she tried to tell him how hurt she was about the distance he kept, but his response of "Get over it, what's the matter with you?" obviously wounded her to the core.

His words seemed straight out of my father's mouth.

My mother never tried to push him into closer contact again. She was terrified he might not let her see her grandson at all if she did. So, as ever, she kept a low profile when any family discord was aired, and as usual, we resented her for it.

My older sister, Debra, still socially awkward and lacking in self-esteem, even in her mid 40s, found confrontation as difficult as our mother. She tried to stand up for Rob, and the way my mother was behaving, and that angered Jennifer and me too. We simply cut relations.

Debra came out of her shell enough to seek a solution. She found us another counselor. Valerie Morgan was a licensed psychotherapist who specialized in troubled family relationships. So, in the second fall after my father had left us, as the autumn leaves drifted gently from the trees, my mother, Debra, Jennifer and I arrived at an old brick New England house that had been converted into a counseling center.

Rob chose not join the session, claiming there was no need for him to attend as he didn't have any issues. Brian was too far away.

We stepped into the small waiting room, with a rock water fountain and several hanging green plants. Jennifer and I sat on off-white cushioned chairs next to each other and giggled like teenagers, while Debra and my mother sat across the room, quietly flipping the pages of old Readers Digest magazines.

"Shhhhhhhh," my mother placed a finger in front of her mouth, advising Jennifer and me to lower the volume, like we were kids again, and not in our mid thirties.

"Hello, you must be the Sinclairs." Valerie came out to greet us.

She motioned us into her office and towards a large brown suede couch and a matching overstuffed chair. Dressed in a brown skirt and beige sweater with natural brown leather boots, she reminded me of an LL bean model. Her natural look without make up made me trust her almost immediately. Here's someone that's not covering things up, I thought.

Debra nervously sat down in the chair. The twitch in her left eye, which was always obvious when she felt anxious, revealed how uncomfortable she was feeling. She patted her short brown hair with her hands while staring at the floor. My mother sat down at the end of the couch, letting out an audible sigh, as if she was already exhausted from the meeting that hadn't even begun. Jennifer and I landed next to her. We each introduced ourselves and Valerie smiled at each of us.

"Debra, why don't you start? Tell me what I can help you with?"

"I...I...don't...know," Debra responded. "Everything seemed fine until Julia stopped speaking to our brother, Rob."

I wanted to interrupt Debra but stopped myself. She continued. "If you ask Rob, he would say that all this not speaking to him came out of nowhere. But if you ask Jennifer or Julia, they would say something about World War II and I...I...just don't know... Mom wants us all to speak to each other again."

"And what about you Debra? What do you want?"

Jennifer's face became as red as a fire engine, and her green-hazel eyes widened. "She doesn't have an opinion! Have you ever met someone who doesn't have an opinion!? How can someone not have an opinion? You know, that's how the Germans got away with killing six million Jewish people during World War II, because no one had an opinion, just like you Debra!"

Jennifer's pony tail swung back and forth as she turned her body from side to side, making eye contact with each of us. Since seeing the movie 'Schindler's List' Jennifer was often talking about the dangers of silence and the consequences of not taking action when atrocities were being committed.

Jennifer would bring up Auschwitz and Hitler, when trying to make her points, but most people, like Debra and my mother, would not make the philosophical connection. They would instead jump to the conclusion that Jennifer was comparing them to Adolph Hitler, and then any discussion would descend into rage.

"Jennifer, let your sister speak and we'll hear from you afterwards." Valerie gestured for Jennifer to calm down.

"Debra!" Jennifer muttered, shaking her head.

Debra sank deeper into the chair and didn't look up from the floor. But Valerie kept looking at her, and waiting, until she finally looked up. "Are you all set Debra, is that everything you'd like to say?".

"Yep." Debra nodded and looked at my mother, as if willing the conversation to move away from herself.

Valerie smiled at my mother: "How about you? How do you think I can help your family?"

My mother's short and stocky body looked even more stunted as she sat with shoulders curving forward, and spoke in a frail voice.

"It seems like the only time they all get along is when they are not together. I just want things to be like they used to be. I'm 68 years old. I'm too old for this."

"You want things the way they used to be?" I couldn't keep from interjecting. "So, Mummy, you want to go back to everyone yelling and screaming while you do nothing at all, is that it?"

"Yelling and screaming, screaming and yelling. Why do you twins always have to resort to that? You can't leave the peace, let things be, just let things be. You two have been this way your whole life."

Jennifer's voice erupted like thunder: "That's all you want Mommy…to leave things alone, let things be. Doesn't matter how many people get killed in your eyes, as long as they don't touch you, eh Mommy? You're just as bad as the Germans!"

"Jennifer, you must let your mother speak." Valerie implored.

"Those two, Debra and Mommy, they wouldn't know how to speak if you paid them a million bucks. Peace, peace, peace! That's all they want! Peace at any cost! You can never take a stand, Mommy. You have no backbone!"

Jennifer's words increased in speed as they spilled out of her mouth.

"Well, what is wrong with peace?" My mother started crying. "I can't say anything right…whatever I say, one of you girls always has a problem with it. I can't say anything without getting screamed at."

"So Marjie," Valerie summarized. "You would like your family to get along. I do understand that. Most parents do desire for their children to get along, especially as adults. You aren't living together. You want everyone to get along for the holidays and different times during the year when you see them, I understand."

My mother simply nodded.

Valerie then moved on to Jennifer and me. Jennifer summed up her thinking quickly. "Everything I just said – that's why we are here!"

I tried to summarize the issue, explaining that my mother would continuously accept abuse from Rob, and furthermore, did not have our backs when Rob treated one of us badly, just like she didn't have our backs when we were children and my father was being abusive.

Valerie nodded her head. "Yes, I am interested in when you were children. What were your childhoods like?"

Debra squirmed in her chair and waited. When called upon to speak, she looked up into the air as if she was downloading her memories from our early years.

"Very normal. It was a good childhood. I rode my bike around the neighborhood a lot, I went to the park and swung on the swings, I used to love to do that. And I liked to bounce my basketball in the driveway....yeah, very normal."

I rolled my eyes, Jennifer shook her head, and my mother looked at Debra with a straight face. I could not read my mother's expression. At that moment, I remembered many other times when I couldn't read my mother's expression. My mother's face was often without expression, during what other people would consider highly emotional exchanges. I suddenly realized it was a mask. I remembered the time she told us about a miscarriage she had had. No expression, no tears.

"Well, miscarriages just happen sometimes," was all she said.

There was another time she told us that our uncle had committed suicide. Again, no expression, no tears. "Your uncle died the way he wanted to," we were told. We never even went to his funeral. Most surprising though was when she talked about my twin's cancer, when Jennifer was three months old.

"Yeah, that line on your stomach, Jennifer, that is where they cut into you to remove the tumors. That was the only time I've ever seen your father cry." But again she showed no expression, no tears.

I tried again now to read my mother's face. Nothing. She was just accepting that Debra had left out years and years of in-family fighting? Did my mother not remember the violence? Was she waiting until it was her turn?

Jennifer did not have a straight face. Her forehead crinkled as her mouth opened wide, although no words initially came out. After about 20 seconds, she was able to say: "Debra, what the hell are you talking about? What house were you brought up in? It certainly wasn't ours! Do you not remember the fights, the cops, Daddy beating us all up? Why are you being so stupid?"

Jennifer's bitter sarcasm and name calling often sounded just like my father's. My mother always said they didn't get along because she was too much like him.

"Jennifer, you don't need to call Debra stupid," said Valerie. "She just has different memories. Tell me what you remember."

After a deep breath, Jennifer started.

"Well, Daddy used to holler and yell and hit us, and we used to scream and yell back, and Mommy was just like she is now. She couldn't stop it....or wouldn't stop it. Mommy, I didn't cause those fights!" She glared at my mother and then looked back at

Valerie, "Later, when I was in high school, I found whiskey hidden behind his books on the shelves ......and places like that."

"And in the rafters in the ceiling of the basement. Remember Jennifer?" I added.

"I remember everything. I remember being punched in the stomach and being unable to breathe. I remember the knife. I remember him grabbing my fist and not allowing me to let go but him screaming at me to let it go. He was crazy. I would never ever hit a child. I would kill anyone that tried to hurt my daughter." Jennifer's eyes teared up as she mentioned her newly-adopted baby girl.

"Samantha is one year old, but you girls were old enough to protect yourselves." My mother looked over and gave Jennifer and me a disgusted look. "And Jennifer, you cut your father's leather money belt. I do remember that."

"We were not yet ten years old? You believe we were old enough to defend ourselves against a 45 year-old man? Really Mummy? You are still defending him now and he is dead?"

Tears welled up in my mother's eyes. "What are you thinking right now, Marjie?" Valerie asked.

"The girls, especially Jennifer, show no respect for their father what-so-ever. Walter was so proud of you kids, going to college and all of you graduating....and now this, never any respect."

"So Marjie, your husband – Walter - had an issue with alcohol?" Valerie asked for confirmation.

"He liked his drink now and then, but it wasn't like that." My mother pulled a tissue out of a box on the table.

"Wasn't like what?" Valerie leaned forward.

"You're going to say he was an alcoholic....or something...."

"Sounds like he had a problem, if he was hitting his children and there was alcohol hidden throughout the house."

"He was not an alcoholic," my mother said, as she wiped tears from her eyes.

"Why do you say that?" Valerie squinted.

"Alcoholics live under bridges and drink from brown paper bags – that was not their father. Their father went to work every day....every single day." She looked at Jennifer and then at me, as tears rolled down her cheeks. "I can't believe you're speaking about your father like this. You won't even allow the poor guy to rest in peace."

"Marjie, I'm not saying your husband didn't love his children, but it sounds like he was addicted to alcohol, and Jennifer especially didn't behave as you would have liked her to when he drank."

"Those two, those two," my mother sniffled. "Jennifer and Walter, they were just too much alike. That's what caused so many fights, and it was also the full moon, Jennifer would always start in when the moon was full."

I heard Jennifer laugh with derision at my side.

"Marjie, it does sound like it was the alcohol that was behind the fights."

My mother shook her head.

"Functioning alcoholics are able to hold down jobs," Valerie explained. "Many do very well at professional jobs, while "needing" alcohol to relax. Many deny drinking, hide their alcohol, and become angry and defensive if confronted about it."

She was describing my father to a "T". This was a revelation to me. Looking back now I suppose it seems obvious to the reader. But we were blinded by our closeness.

"Jennifer, Julia. You poked the bear throughout your childhood. You weren't "supposed to" poke the bear. When your father was drinking it seems you would confront him, get in his way, but in your father's state of mind, under the influence of the alcohol, he wasn't capable of being the parent you needed." I looked at her and nodded.

My mother's eyes were as red as an albino mouse. I looked at her as she shook her head back and forth. Somehow, it didn't feel right allowing my mother, who always saw herself as the victim, to feel even more pain, but in other ways, it felt one hundred percent right.

This was the first time in my life that I felt either Jennifer or I were being validated. I had known my whole life that something wasn't right, and now I understood that it didn't start with Jennifer or me, or any of my siblings. We were finally being told the truth and everything started to make sense.

The subject of my brother Rob's abusive personality was not discussed until a few sessions later, but this was the first piece of a very large jigsaw puzzle that went back generations, and had even led me to marry a person just as emotionally and verbally abusive as my father.

CHAPTER 16
LEARNING ABOUT THE DEATHS

"It's incredibly dangerous to leave an abuser, because the final step in the domestic violence pattern is: Kill her."

– Leslie Morgan Steiner, AMERICAN AUTHOR AND
ADVOCATE FOR WOMEN'S RIGHTS

I felt only a little guilty as I typed in my sister's email and Facebook password to get into her account. She had provided it to me two years before, when I was using my phone to show her how to upload a photo. I had remembered the password ever since and I had used it periodically to get into her account. I rationalized that I was just making sure I was aware of comments being made about me by family members which I wasn't linked to.

I clicked on her "friends", knowing that she was linked with my mother, Rob and my sister-in- law. I had distanced myself from them all, but she hadn't.

I was still confused and offended by my brothers' desire to be friends with my ex-husband. I trawled through my sister-in-law's post of her wedding day. They had been married 23 years now, 20 years since my divorce, but she always posted the same pictures on her anniversary. I noted that Randy had not commented on the pictures this year. I wondered if he had grown bored of seeing them. There was nothing else from Randy on any of their posts. I looked at his profile and there were no new posts going some time.

I turned to Google and typed Randy's name and the word 'arrest' into the search field. I wondered if he might have done something and no one had told me.

Immediately, images popped up on the iPad screen. None of them were him. I clicked on "all" in order to see more, and saw one link with his name, on a website called BUSTEDNEWSPAPER.com. It reported that a Randy Christopher Castleton had been arrested.

"Oh My God." I paused for a moment.

It listed a date as part of the identification number of the person arrested. It was Randy's birthday. It had to be him.

I saw the world "burglary" and the information that a bond amount had been set at $50,000. I began to doubt it was the same Randy. He would never rob anyone. But then a chill went down my spine as I saw "First Degree Murder" higher up the page. I clicked on it. There was a picture of a curly-haired man, one of the same pictures I had seen when I first put his name in the search engine. For a moment I was truly relieved. It was just a bizarre coincidence. But then I looked closer.

Holy Shit! That was him. I stared at his eyes. They looked crazed in the mug shot.

This wasn't burglary; this was murder. Of a woman. Probably a female he had felt betrayed by; who had withdrawn her love from him. I was jumping to conclusions, but my mind was racing as I tried to take in all the information.

I remembered his desperation. His tears. All the times he had said "I can't live without you". Who was his victim? I needed to know. Who was this woman who could so easily have been me?

I suddenly felt filled with guilt at a conversation I had had with my mother when we were separated.

"I just want him to find someone else to obsess over," I had explained.

"How can you say that? You are his wife. You shouldn't be wishing he will find someone else."

I had known that once he fell for another woman, I would truly be free.

"Springfield police have obtained a murder warrant for the ex-boyfriend of Sandra Davis Wilson, who was found shot dead in her home on Monday night. Her ex-boyfriend, Randy Christopher Castleton, of Arlington, remains hospitalized with 'significant self-inflicted injuries'. Police also obtained a warrant charging Castleton with burglary."

The report said he had still been at the scene with his victim's body as police arrived but had been transported directly to the hospital.

The date on the report showed it had been a year since the killing.

I found out that he had been on remand in prison, ever since being released from the hospital the prior summer. He hadn't been tried yet, but the evidence was so convincing it seemed certain that he would now spend many years in prison.

I wondered if his self-inflicted injuries had been his attempt to take his own life, and if he was sorry he had not been successful.

The pictures in the newspaper report showed a white sheet hung over the front door of the house. Had he beaten the door in, with a gun in his hand, to get to her? I imagined how frightened she must have been. Had she tried to escape? Hoped for rescue?

I stayed up late that night looking up as much information on the case as I could.

She was the mother of two grown-up children. Both her parents were in their nineties. There were 195 pictures on the family obituary website. Randy had been dating her but the relationship had broken up.

If it was possible to have survivor guilt for someone you didn't know, I had it.

I know I had wanted him to find someone else, but I didn't want that person to die! Had I done enough to try to stop a future murder? Hadn't I just walked out on him and not looked back? All the signs of his instability had been there. That was why I had been afraid he would eventually kill someone. Should I have told someone?

And it wasn't just her. It was just more obvious this time.

Jennifer and I had discovered two years before that Randy had remarried, but his second wife had died young. We had found that out on Facebook.

The morning after his wife had died, Randy had posted a picture on his timeline of women's buttocks, along with a joke saying that women with large buttocks will have smart children. He had written below it that he would love to have a lot of smart children. His wife had not even been dead twenty- four hours, and this did not seem like the behavior of a grieving widow. It had sent a chill down my spine.

"He killed her," Jennifer said.

"Yes, I know......." I agreed.

I googled his name and his wife's name to see if there was any mention of foul play, but there wasn't.

All my instincts were screaming that there was something wrong, but there was nothing to prove our suspicions.

"We have to call the police, Julia."

"I'm afraid he's going to come after me if he finds out I did that." I didn't want to risk having to be anywhere near Randy again.

"Then I will report it." I couldn't stop her, and it actually felt good to have someone caring enough to do something for me. That was rare.

Jennifer spoke to the police station close to where Randy and his wife had lived and suggested that they might want to investigate her death. She was told that an autopsy had already been completed and it did not show that Barbara Castleton had been killed. She had apparently died of an overdose. This did not make me feel much better. What sort of state must she have been in to want to take her own life?

Jennifer was still talking to the officer.

"Are you sure, officer, because I truly believe that her husband is capable of murder."

"What makes you think that?" I heard him say on the speaker phone.

"Because I know the guy!" Jennifer shot back faster than a bullet.

"Listen. I know the guy too. I've had to put him in his place a few times. I'm not saying he didn't drive her to it, but we don't think it's murder."

Jennifer hung up the phone and we looked at each other. There was nothing more to be done.

Now I sat, wondering, would I have been the one who committed suicide or the one shot in her own home? Instead I was the one who had got away.

If Randy and I had had children, they would have been the same age as the two young adults his ex-girlfriend had just left behind. They would have ended up with no mom and no real dad - one dead and one in prison. It didn't bear thinking about.

CHAPTER 17
LEARNING ABOUT BORDERLINE PERSONALITY DISORDER

"Education is the most powerful weapon which you can use to change the world."

– **Nelson Mandela,** SOUTH AFRICAN ANTI-APARTHEID REVOLUTIONARY,
POLITICAL LEADER, PEACE ACTIVIST AND PHILANTHROPIST

I tried to put the discovery behind me and move on. I tried so hard to forget the awful fate of his ex-girlfriend and focus on my life with Ed. Our little family of two dogs in our cozy house was perfect. Ed's relaxed attitude and trust in my judgement made him the type of person anyone would want for a spouse.

I tried not to think about Randy's situation at all. But it was always there, like a ghost in my mind. Every time I had a moment to myself it crowded forward. All the 'what ifs'. Like a trash bag full of garbage ready for the dump, I wanted to throw the past away and never think about it again; but my mind would not let me.

I remembered a time, shortly after our wedding, when we were both feeling positive about life and our future. We were leaving a friend's barbecue, after an excellent cook-out on a hot August evening. The afternoon had been filled with lawn games, drinking beer from coolers and much laughter. As Randy slid into the driver's seat he smiled at me.

"I wish my old therapist could see me now."

"Your old therapist?" I raised my eyebrows at him. "Why were you seeing a therapist?"

"Oh depression, emptiness. I didn't realize that I just needed to get out of the relationship I was in. She didn't do anything wrong, I just felt empty." He looked at me and shrugged his shoulders.

"And, why do you wish that therapist could see you now?"

"Oh, because he said I had Borderline Personality Disorder. What an asshole."

"Borderline Personality Disorder? You?" I thought about the Borderline patients I had to deal with at the community health center; low functioning adults who needed help with daily life skills and had difficulty separating reality from their imagination. That was not like Randy. Before the wedding Randy had, of course, been unstable, but things were better now and he had calmed down.

"He didn't know what the hell he was talking about!" Randy was going on. "If he could see me now; having a great life, happily married, with lots of friends and a Masters degree! He was so full of shit. I know more now than he ever did!"

I had rolled down my window, turned the music up loud, and watched the pine trees in New Hampshire whizz by. It wasn't something I had wanted to entertain then.

But now, years later, I was still putting the pieces together.

I had known that Borderline Personality Disorder was characterized by emotional instability. But now I wanted to know more. Perhaps you are reading this book because you also want to know more.

I researched endlessly online.

The explanation of the diagnosis in the Diagnostic and Statistical Manual of Mental Disorders said the following:

"A pervasive pattern of instability in interpersonal relationships, poor self-image, and marked impulsivity beginning by early adulthood, and present in a variety of contexts, as indicated by five (or more) of the following:

(1) frantic efforts to avoid real or imagined abandonment

Well, that was certainly true for Randy. He was terrified of abandonment. All the worst moments in our relationship had arisen when he had felt abandoned. And he had certainly acted frantically. I thought about his adrenaline-filled drives between New Hampshire and Florida on zero sleep. I realized he had actually left me first, to avoid the chance of my leaving him.

(2) a pattern of unstable and intense interpersonal relationships, characterized by alternating between extremes of idealization and devaluation

Unstable relationships and alternating extremes. Randy had bounced back and forth between hating me and loving me. I remembered his rampages, his ripping up everything in my apartment — and then welcoming me back from vacation with red roses. The manual called this "splitting". In his eyes, I had been either all good, or all evil; there was no in between.

(3) identity disturbance: markedly and persistently unstable self image or sense of self

Yes, I thought, now his cocky behavior, mixed with his tears, made sense. He had no clear sense of who he was. Sometimes he was the arrogant man, sure that everything he did was right, and sometimes he was the victim, as he had often portrayed himself to my mother after our separation.

(4) impulsivity in at least two areas that are potentially self-damaging (e.g., spending, sex, substance abuse, reckless driving, binge eating).

I recalled Anna telling me about his cheating during his trip to Maine. I remembered her words: "Julia, there's more, but I don't want to divulge it." What had she known that I hadn't? Our sex life had been good but it seemed Randy needed extra-marital sex too. It had made no sense to me then, but now it did. There was a void in him, a weakness, he was constantly trying to fill.

(5) recurrent suicidal behavior, gestures, or threats, or self-mutilating behavior

"I have considered just ending it all," Randy had said to me after we split up. "But I know that wouldn't fix anything." I had considered his words a ploy, to try to get me to feel sorry for him. But the news report about his ex-girlfriend had said he was suffering self-inflicted injuries. Had he tried to kill himself after shooting her?

(6) affective instability due to a marked reactivity of mood (e.g., intense episodic dysphoria, irritability, or anxiety usually lasting a few hours and only rarely more than a few days)

Randy's irritable and anxiety-filled episodes were a consistent feature of our relationship. It was the one constant in our marriage. His irritability matched my father's irritability when he had had a drink.

(7) chronic feelings of emptiness

Looking back, I realized he was always trying to 'find himself'. He had said he felt empty, to his first therapist. He had chopped and changed in relationships when a woman did not fulfill him completely. He was always job hopping; constantly trying to better himself in terms of education. He never seemed to be content with himself or with his life. He constantly needed more.

(8) inappropriate, intense anger or difficulty controlling anger (e.g., frequent displays of temper, constant anger, recurrent physical fights)

Randy had been so full of anger. His temper tantrums were like those of a two year-old, but in the body of an adult.

(9) transient, stress-related paranoid ideation or severe dissociative symptoms

As my mind came full circle, the planned Florida trip came back to me. I had packed up everything in my life to move to Florida with him. He still believed that I was leaving him. There was no logic to his thinking whatsoever. There was no connection to reality.

A diagnosis required five out of the nine traits, and in my mind Randy had all nine. Tic-tac-toe across the entire grid. X's in every box. The real question when we parted should not have been if it would happen, but when.

I plowed through article after article. Each put forward different reasons for the onset of Borderline symptoms, which could become homicidal. One said it was the result of a build-up of psychological tension from an unresolved emotional conflict for which an act of violence provided relief.

Yes, I thought to myself, that is exactly what happened to Randy. It made perfect sense to me that he had killed out of rage; out of hurt; out of desperation, to get some relief.

He had always felt better, and acted more calmly, after he had exploded at me. His explosive outbursts were his relief mechanism. They left me hurt and angry, but once he had released the emotional tension it was over for him.

Jealousy, fear, hate, anger, rejection, depression, hopelessness and embarrassment are all emotions murderers have expressed as an explanation when convicted of their crime.

Randy harbored all these emotions. Furthermore, he blamed me for them. I realized he was a ticking time bomb when I married him, and I had been lucky to get away before he went bang.

CHAPTER 18
MAKING SENSE OF IT ALL

"Memory without the emotional charge is called Wisdom"

—**Joe Dispenza,** NEUROSCIENTIST; INTERNATIONAL TEACHER, LECTURER AND AUTHOR

So I married a murderer.

In hindsight, the red flags on Randy's path to homicide were as visible as wands identifying a snow-covered trail. But only in retrospect.

I berated myself for not seeing it at that time. It was not as if I was a naive teenager. I was in my mid-twenties with a university education. But things had happened in my life which had preconditioned me not to see those markers. The more I read the more I understood what those factors were.

Love Bombing - Like most people, when I fell in love, I fell hard. But because I had received so little overt love when I was small, I needed it more than most. When I met Randy and he showered me with compliments, flowers, gifts, and attention I was so deeply in love with him that he could do virtually anything and I would not leave him. I was dependent. Looking back, his attentiveness was probably a form of manipulation, but I saw it as true, romantic, love.

Perception of Normalcy with Instability and Rage — I had been brought up in a family that was always fighting, so sudden changes of mood and explosive temper were not alien to me. In a way, when Randy and I were fighting, it just felt like home. It was normal to my subconscious mind.

Perception of Normalcy with the "Caretaker" role - I had always been the caretaker to my mother. In the middle of family rows I would always try to shield her from further hurt. I realized I had simply switched from taking care of my mother's feelings to taking care of Randy's, at the expense of my own. I was groomed as a 'caretaker'. However the role was essentially that of unpaid therapist, and I had sacrificed my own well-being. My mother was the archetypal 'caretaker' to my father, and expected me to be the same to Randy. That is why I always felt such pressure to please her.

Trained to Tolerate Abuse from Spouse – I had watched my father abuse my mother throughout my life. He didn't hit her, like he did his children, but he would verbally and emotionally abuse her, especially when he was drunk. I remembered the endless refrain: "Jesus Christ Marjie! Open your goddam eyes. You can't do anything right, can you?" He would still be hollering at her as she ran around trying to please him. He constantly told her she was incompetent and stupid. My mother excelled at covering up the dysfunctionality of our home environment to visitors. I talked about this at length with Valerie the therapist. I said I truly didn't understand why she hadn't left my father, and why she had been so keen I stay with Randy. Her response was very thought-provoking. She said if my mother had accepted that Randy's behavior was unacceptable, she would have had to admit that she should have left my father. Her motives were not malicious. She had trained me to tolerate abuse because she wanted me to have love.

The Drama Triangle – Our life, when I was young, was always a drama, and generally negative. I had got used to the dysfunctional role-play in our household. When I married Randy I was simply swapping one dysfunctional environment for another. Our relationship was 'The Perfect Storm'. A man, afraid of being abandoned with a co-dependent-in-training.

It was obvious I had been brought up by a mother in denial. But I didn't need to follow her lead.

"In her mind, Julia, your mother thinks she's telling the truth," said Valerie in one of our sessions. "When she tells you she doesn't remember, she doesn't. When she remembers your sister and you "back-talking" her, that is easier than accepting your father's excessive alcohol use. As a parent, it was her responsibility to keep you safe, and she didn't do that. She actually couldn't do that, because she saw herself as a victim too. It is far too painful for her to acknowledge that she didn't protect you, so her subconscious blocks it out. She blames you so she doesn't have to blame herself."

I once heard my mother say to Jennifer: "I didn't take either side. I think I was pretty much neutral."

In my mind neutral was not something to be lauded, but a dereliction of duty.

I did wonder what she really thought about all those times she had begged me to stay with Randy, only to be confronted with the brutal truth that he was a murderer.

Perhaps she might say that he had only become one because I had not stood loyally beside him. When Jennifer gave her the news about the killing of his ex-girlfriend, all she said was: "I don't remember much of that."

She had that luxury, but I didn't.

EPILOGUE

As I started putting all of these pieces together, half a century into my life, I remembered a pleasant Sunday afternoon when I was young and my father was polishing his collection of rifles as he listened to Marty Robbins "El Paso" on the cabinet-sized stereo in the living room.

I loved calm Sunday afternoons and I knew that when Daddy was polishing guns he was never mean Daddy; he was always nice Daddy. I sat on the corner of the footstool where he rested his legs.

"Daddy?" I looked up at him. "Tell me what it was like when you were my age."

"Oh dear, that was a long time ago," he laughed. But he then grew more serious, as he explained: "When I walked to school, it was much longer than your walk. It was a long slog, and when we got home there were chores to do, and if we didn't do those chores right our daddy would whip us until we did. And if he had had a drink or two we would hide, in case he came after us to deliver another beating."

I remember thinking that was terrible, but I strangely never made the connection as a child that my father did the same thing. Or that both my father, and his father were alcoholics.

I began to understand why Aunt Mary had left the family home and never gone back. Then I recognized how my own family, as adults, had repeated the same dysfunctional family dynamic.

Rob had withdrawn, like Mary, taking his son with him, and Brian had put miles between us all. Debra had never really emerged. My twin sister had chosen someone identical to my father, and indeed she used to describe him as "just like drunk Daddy".

Randy was now behind bars, probably for the remainder of his life. I doubted his perspective had changed much. But the undefined traumas he had experienced as a child had shaped his life, just as those we had experienced had shaped ours.

It has taken me fifty years of hardship and heartbreak to even begin to understand the human condition. But I have years left yet to get it right. Life is a journey. Some of us get derailed at the start, but we can all get our engine back on the rails, and just keep going.

That is what is truly expected of us.

AFTERWORD
June, 2019

Randy Christopher Castleton, aged 61, pleaded guilty to second degree murder on June 27th, 2019 for killing 54 year-old Sandra Davis Wilson in July of 2016.

The court was told that three days before her murder Randy had purchased a 20 gauge shotgun. He wrapped it in an American flag, and then forced his way into his ex-girlfriend's home as her son tried to keep the door closed. He shot her twice, once in the chest and once in the head. While her son ran to the neighbors for help, Randy stabbed himself with a hunting knife. He was carrying a suicide note.

Prosecutors shared key parts of the suicide note at the hearing. He had opened the letter with: 'I win. I win.' He wrote: "If I can't have what I want, then I will cause pain for as many people as I can." It seemed Randy's main regret was leaving his dogs behind. "I hate leaving my dogs," he went on. "I don't mind killing Sandra because she deserved it, and… if she had never opened the gate to this then it never would have happened."

Randy was sentenced to the maximum jail time for second degree murder; 25-31 years.

His lawyers had insisted he was suffering from diminished capacity due to mental health issues and the recent suicide of his late wife.

He will be 84 years old before being eligible for parole.

A news report on the court case explained that Randy and Sandra had only dated briefly. Close friends of Sandra said that Randy was unhappy that her kids were more important to her than he was. He was not happy about the relationship ending.

Randy's lawyer said his action had been inconsistent with "how he led his life."

They didn't know Randy as I knew Randy.

CPSIA information can be obtained
at www.ICGtesting.com
Printed in the USA
FFHW010205111019
55440925-61249FF